WHAT AM I GOING TO DO?

How To Prepare For An IMPENDING DIVORCE

Tips From A Board Certified Texas Family Law Attorney

Attorney William D. Bloodworth II

Speakeasy Publishing

73-03 Bell Blvd, #10

Oakland Gardens, NY 11364

www.speakeasypublishinginc.com

Ordering Information:

Quantity sales. Special discounts are available on quantity purchases by corporations, associations, and others. For details, contact the publisher at the address above.

Orders by U.S. trade bookstores and wholesalers. Please contact Speakeasy Publishing: Tel: (888) 991-2766 or visit www.speakeasypublishinginc.com.

Printed in the United States of America

Published in 2019

ISBN: 978-1-946481-79-5

FOREWORD

Why I Do What I Do

In 1987, while serving as pastor of a church, I became engaged to a young woman I had grown up knowing, but who attended another church in my hometown. We married and were soon expecting our first child. Shortly after we were married, and before my daughter was born, my wife told me she wanted a divorce. I was devastated. We had both been raised in church and taught that divorce was wrong. One day I came home from work, and almost everything in the house was gone! The washing machine was sitting in the front yard. The only reason it was not also gone was because my wife ran out of time to remove it before I returned home from work! My wife had left me! She was six months pregnant with our daughter Rachel. Later, I was not allowed to be present at Rachel's birth. I was heartbroken. My whole world had been turned upside down. I didn't know what to do or where to turn.

I did not want a divorce, but I quickly found out that in Texas, if your spouse wants a divorce, they can get one--whether you want it or not. My wife wanted one; she filed for divorce and requested custody of our daughter. Our divorce was a bitter one. My wife would not talk to me unless she was in court on the witness stand. She was silent as we exchanged our daughter at visitations. When my wife got a new boyfriend, I had to deliver my child to him at visitations (when my now ex-wife) sent him.

When my daughter Rachel was about 2 1/2 years old, my ex-wife and I were scheduled for court on a Motion to Modify Visitation. My wife began to talk to me because she did not want me to take my daughter to Virginia for my extended summer period of possession. We continued talking and discussed what was "in the child's best interest." Those discussions, along with a miracle of God, resulted in my wife and I getting remarried. My wife, my daughter, and I returned to Virginia where I was in my last year of law school. We finished law school together: as a family.

After graduation from law school, I returned to Texas and began my practice of law in Livingston. In 1993, I moved to Huntsville, Texas and began practicing law. Since that time, I have engaged in a general practice of law, which involves all kinds of legal cases, but I have a strong interest and personal fondness for the practice of family law--especially divorce and child custody cases.

I have not forgotten what it is like to hand my child over to a stranger at visitation. I have not forgotten what it was like to have my stomach in knots with the worry and stress of dealing with a person I once loved and now can't stand. I know what it's like to just seem to argue over the smallest of details. I know what it's like to want information regarding my child and not to be able to get any cooperation from the other parent.

That's why I do what I do: practicing law, fighting for what is right and opposing what is wrong!

DEDICATION

This book is dedicated to God, "The Lawgiver." With God, all things are possible, and you God, kept your word to me and have blessed me to see many impossible things become a reality in my life.

"20 You, who have shown me great and severe troubles,
Shall revive me again,
And bring me up again from the depths of the earth.
21 You shall increase my greatness,
And comfort me on every side."

– Psalm 71:20-21 (NKJV)

Next, I dedicate this book to my first and second wife, Deanna; the love of my life! You have loved me, stood by me, advised me, and inspired me. My favorite place on earth is: wherever you are. You are extremely intelligent, gifted, attentive to details, a very hard worker, and everyone's favorite, especially mine.

Next, to my children, **Rachel**, my "little lawyer," who God used to bring Deanna and me back together again; who has grown up to follow me in the legal profession, so capable now, and I cannot wait to see what you do in the future. **Scarlett**, a God seeker, strong, full of integrity; a determined one for whom "failure is not an option." **Victoria**, my "on fleek", a beautiful smile, the brains to go with it, and a very hard worker; "You've come a long way, baby."

Next, I dedicate this book to my mother Rita, who has always believed in me, even when others did not. The one who fought for me, and who has been my biggest fan, always. You taught me "to thine own self be true," "be sure your sins will find you out." You taught me to appreciate the "finer things of life," developed within me an appreciation for history, culture, and cultivated me into the man I have become.

Finally, to my "mother-in-love" Velma, one of my best friends. One person who truly knows the love of God and how to live it out, every day. You are smart and very perceptive. You have taught me compassion for the lost, and the power of a fearless witness. You serve as an example for me to live up to.

ACKNOWLEDGEMENTS

Deanna and Rachel, for your inspiration and contributions in subject matter ideas, editing, and proofreading.

Tina Markham, for content suggestions, photo illustration suggestions, and proofreading.

Blaire Midgett, for holding down the fort while I was working on this project, and for your help editing.

Reed Midgett, for editing the manuscript, except for the Chapter on CPS-- and we all know why.

Angela Gaston, my sister, for coming to my rescue, and doing the final edit. Thank you!

Scarlett Bloodworth, my daughter for editing the editor's edit, and your gift of attention to detail.

Carl J. Stevens, Esq., without you, I wouldn't have been able to practice law!

Prof. Herbert W. Titus, my beloved Dean, who taught me Constitutional law from a biblical foundation; and who continues to impress and inspire me.

DISCLAIMER

This publication is intended to be used for educational purposes only. No legal advice is being given, and no attorney-client relationship is intended to be created by reading this material. The author assumes no liability for any errors or omissions or for how this book or its contents are used or interpreted or for any consequences resulting directly or indirectly from the use of this book. For legal or any other advice, please consult an experienced attorney or the appropriate expert who is aware of the specific facts of your case and is knowledgeable of the law in your jurisdiction.

Certain instances of grammatical form have been intentionally used, and some grammatical errors (especially in the testimonials) have not been corrected to maintain the truth and integrity of these unsolicited testimonials, as they were originally written by the clients themselves. Certain forms of proper legal citation and abbreviation have been omitted or changed, for it to be understood by more people. Citations have been used with the idea and purpose to assist the untrained to understand and decipher the citation and to quickly obtain the source material.

Bloodworth Law Firm, PLLC.

William Douglas Bloodworth II
303 Longmire Road
Suite 1002
Conroe, TX 77304
www.bloodworthlawfirm.com
(936) 291-3100

Testimonials

(Notice: These are actual reviews written by actual clients, no spelling correction or grammar corrections have been made.)

"Gave me great advice. I've dealt with my custody case the past five plus years and his law firm has NEVER let me down. His staff, Tina and Blaire, are absolutely amazing and go above and beyond to help like they did me and without whose help I never could've won custody of my child. There are attorneys out there who claim to fight on your behalf, and I have dealt with them, but this guy, unequivocally, is truly the epitome of someone who will get into the ring for you and give it everything he has and more. Without Mr. Bloodworth, I would have never have been able to win custody of my seven-year-old. You want someone who knows his stuff, and will absolutely annihilate the other party with his strategy, eloquence, and evidence, then you hire William Bloodworth. You'd be glad you did and sorry if you didn't." ***— Affan***

****

"The Bloodworth Law Firm, including its excellent staff, recently handled a long, drawn-out divorce suit, not of my making. We have no information on why the divorce was initiated or what the other side wanted out of the settlement. All the issues were handled by the Bloodworth firm with professionalism and compassion. My situation and well-being were considered throughout the process. The other side was not forthcoming with information but the Bloodworth Law Firm persisted in gathering what information was required. A reason for the divorce was never provided. William Bloodworth and his friendly and supportive staff completed the divorce process in a fair and just manner. I would recommend the Bloodworth Law Firm to anyone who is looking for legal assistance." ***— Laurence***

****

"Mr. Bloodworth and his staff helped me work through the process of leaving and overcoming an emotionally and physically abusive relationship, while maintaining both the safety of my young daughter and myself. Mr. Bloodworth, Rachel, and Tina were not only professionally available but also personal and understanding of the difficult time I was going through. They took the time to explain and listen to me as well as help me understand the severity of my situation when fear dictated my thoughts and I had lost all sense of normalcy. My emails and calls were returned within hours (usually within the hour) and my questions were always thoroughly addressed and answers explained. Mr. Bloodworth and his staff stood by my side for over a year and I will forever be grateful for the integral part they played in ensuring the best possible outcome was achieved for me and my daughter."

— Jessica

****

"Mr. Bloodworth truly knows how to practice law. I have used him for a divorce, a criminal defense case and to prepare my Estate Plan. He truly understands how to work for his clients and his staff is top notch! Mr. Bloodworth worked diligently to prepare my divorce case for trial, his staff prepared the case and appropriate notebooks perfectly! Mr. Bloodworth defended me with rigor in my criminal case. His staff, Annette and Rachel are wonderful; they are always helpful and seem to understand my case better than I do. If I were a lawyer, I would want Annette and Rachel working in my office. Mr. Bloodworth prepared my will within 4 days."

— A Satisfied Client

****

"Mr. Bloodworth had helped me with getting custody of my granddaughter and was amazing to our family and very aware of documentation in court. He cared so much for us as his client. Mr. Bloodworth years ago helped us with an adoption and was awesome at that time and I will always use and recommend Mr. Bloodworth to friends and family!!!!!"

— Christina and Jimmie

****

TABLE OF CONTENTS

About the Author

I was born and raised a Texan and grew up in Livingston, Polk County, Texas. I graduated from Livingston High School and attended Southwestern Assemblies of God University, where I graduated with a Bachelor of Science in Pastoral Ministries. I began as an associate pastor in Livingston with my father, who was the pastor of Gethsemane Chapel. I assisted my father in his ministry in Livingston for some time and then I became pastor of that same church.

About a year after becoming pastor, my church merged with another church in Livingston. I then joined the United States

Navy Reserves and attended Regent University School of Law, where I graduated in 1992 with a Juris Doctorate degree. I was admitted to practice law by the Supreme Court of Texas in November of 1992, and I opened my practice in Livingston, Texas. I founded what was then known as William D. Bloodworth II, Attorney and Counselor at Law, which I later formed as a professional limited liability company. Shortly thereafter, I began doing an extensive amount of work with the Texas prison system, in which I was assigned responsibility for all inmate requests for legal assistance in the women's prison units in Texas, which generated a large amount of family law related legal work.

Often, women sentenced to prison have minor children who need to be cared and provided for during their mother's incarceration. There was an extensive amount of family law work in transitioning those children from the care of the parent, who had become incarcerated, to other family members and individuals who could care for them in the incarcerated parent's absence. There was a significant amount of litigation regarding child support and the parental rights of parents who had become incarcerated. I very quickly learned the "ins and outs" of family law. I maintained my private practice while working for the Texas prison system.

Working for the prison system took me all over the state of Texas, handling inmates' cases wherever they might be incarcerated or have litigation involving them. This season of working with the Texas Prison System gave me a wide variety of court experience all over the state of Texas. I have been a lawyer since 1992 and I practice all types of litigation other than bankruptcy and tax law. I enjoy "the battle in the courtroom" and I have a strong passion for family law. I am board certified in family law by the Texas Board of Legal Specialization. Less than 1% of all Texas lawyers are board certified in family law by the Texas Board of Legal Specialization.

I am the founding attorney of the Bloodworth Law Firm, PLLC. For over 26 years, I have practiced as a trial attorney. I have tried all kinds of cases but I was drawn to family law because of my own personal experience of going through an unwanted divorce.

Because of my own experience with a bitter divorce, (see the Forward of this book, page 3) I have a unique understanding of the impact a divorce takes on people, and the emotional toll it takes on every member of the family. I have never forgotten what divorce feels like. It is because of this life experience that I am drawn to and have a special affinity for family law cases.

CHAPTER 1

WHAT AM I GOING TO DO?
CONCERNS THAT PEOPLE HAVE WHEN CONTEMPLATING DIVORCE

1. WHAT WILL HAPPEN TO OUR KIDS?

The first concern of divorcing parents is what is going to happen to their kids. If a parent has custody and wants to maintain that custody, they're concerned because they want to do what it takes to not lose custody. Also, there seems to be, in my experience, a great misunderstanding of what "full custody," or its correct name "conservatorship" means, especially in Texas, because there are so many different variations of conservatorship. Conservatorship will be discussed more fully in Chapter 7 of this book.

If a parent cannot seek to be named the conservator with the right to establish the primary residence of the child (often referred to as "managing" custody of their children) they're usually concerned about the amount of child support they will have to pay and what type of visitation they will have with their children. Many parents, to a large degree, don't mind paying child support--they just don't want to pay more than the law requires, or more than they can afford to pay.

2. DO I HAVE TO LEAVE OUR HOME?

People are also concerned about whether they're going to be evicted by their spouse from their marital residence and on what terms and conditions they can be forced to leave their home. Another concern people have is what will happen to their house and property. If they do leave, does the other person get the house and property? If so, on what terms? Who is going to pay which bills of the family's household during the divorce case? What is the definition of "fair"? Another primary concern is the price of the divorce itself and who will pay for it.

3. WHAT DO I DO IF I DON'T KNOW WHERE MY SPOUSE IS?

Some of the most common misconceptions people have about divorce is that they must get the permission of their spouse to obtain a divorce. Many people believe that if they don't get the other spouse's permission or cooperation, they can't get a divorce.

While not knowing the physical whereabouts of a spouse is problematic, a spouse may still obtain a divorce even if they don't know where their spouse is located. The law has a process for obtaining a divorce even if you have lost track of your spouse and don't know where they are.

Often, couples separate and don't immediately file for divorce. Years will pass and they will start "new lives," but they don't realize the legal implications of that "new life." They may have moved on, but the law in Texas still views anything they purchase as community property, (half) owned by the other spouse. This can be very problematic from a liability standpoint.

For instance, suppose that you have separated from your spouse and have moved on with your life. Your spouse lives with someone else and has a new job but is driving a vehicle that is titled in your name because, when you were a couple, it was financed in your name due to your good credit. When the two of you separated, your spouse took the vehicle. However, your spouse did not purchase insurance for the vehicle, and on top of that, your spouse gets drunk and, while driving, is involved in a collision, which results in the death of another person. Because your name is on the title to the vehicle, you are the vehicle owner and therefore liable for huge damages caused by your "lawful" spouse driving property purchased by the two of you during your marriage, property which is titled in your name. Being liable for a such a large debt that your estranged spouse incurred can negatively affect what you could do in your new life.

People don't think they can get divorced until they find out where their spouse is located. That is simply not the case. The law has a process for obtaining a divorce even if you have lost track of your spouse and don't know where they are.

4. DOES A FATHER HAVE A CHANCE AT GAINING CUSTODY?

Another common misconception is that the mother automatically gets custody of the children. Equal rights have made great progress in our country in recent years. Both parents have equal rights to seek custody of their children and the opportunity to raise their children. I have won custody for men on several occasions. The right man can easily obtain custody. Texas courts must follow the "best interest of the child" standard in determining which parent receives custody.

5. IT'S AN EMERGENCY ! WHY DO I HAVE TO WAIT 60 DAYS?

Another misconception people have about divorce is that their divorce is an "emergency" that deserves the court stopping everything to take immediate notice of what is happening to them. Although they are embroiled, often, in the most turmoil they will ever experience in their lives, that turmoil does not equate to the legal definition of an "emergency." By law, a court does not have lawful authority to grant a divorce until at least 60 days have passed since the divorce has been filed. This mandatory waiting period cannot be waived unless the respondent has been convicted of, or has received deferred adjudication probation for family violence against the person seeking the divorce or a member of that person's household. Otherwise, the petitioner, must have an active Protective Order, Magistrate's Protective Order, or Order for Emergency Protection under the Code of Criminal Procedure. [1]

6. HOW DO I GET A DIVORCE WITHOUT A LAWYER?

Another concern of people contemplating a divorce is not only "what am I going to do," but "how am I going to get it done?" Although you can represent yourself in a Texas divorce suit, that is not advisable. Just because you have a scalpel and *can* cut yourself open does not mean that you can perform surgery on yourself. Many times in an effort to save money, people will represent themselves and leave money on the table or get a very bad verdict or settlement, not because their case lacked merit, but because they represented themselves and didn't know the law, what they were entitled to ask for, or how to present evidence to the court in a format that would have supported their request.

[1] See, Texas Family Code, Section §6.702.(c)

Many people expect the judge to "cut them some slack" because they represent themselves and they're not a lawyer. However, judges cannot take sides in a case. Even though you are not a lawyer, the judge is not allowed by law to act as your lawyer or cut you slack in following the rules of court and evidence. If a judge were to do so, they would cross the line of neutrality and become an advocate for you or your opposition; both would be improper and illegal. President Abraham Lincoln is quoted as saying: "He who represents himself has a fool for a client." You should hire a lawyer to represent you any time you have business before a court. Who you hire to represent you matters a great deal. So, who do you hire?

CHAPTER 2

QUALITIES TO LOOK FOR IN A DIVORCE ATTORNEY

I believe a divorce attorney should be someone who has a passion for family law. You see many lawyers advertise the number of years they've been a lawyer and their vast amount of "experience." You need to interview your potential lawyers. In my office, my paralegals and I work as a team *with* my clients. As a Board-Certified lawyer, I know the law. But my clients know "the facts" of their case, what happened, when it happened, and how it happened. By working together, as a team, we can present the facts and the evidence to the court in such a way that will best persuade the judge or the jury to decide in your favor.

Some lawyers will treat you like just another number. They're not passionate about what's happened to you and what you're going through. Passion and urgency will not come through in their presentation, and presentation is a key component of winning your case. You may have heard the saying, "Court is not about the truth. It's not about what really happened. It's about what you can prove." In court, your lawyer's job is to take what happened to you and weave that into a story, supported by legally admissible evidence, for the judge or jury to consider. You're not going to be able to show the judge everything that happened. You must create a starting point, decide what to show, and where to end the story you present to the court. Knowing what to include in that story, what to leave out of that story, and how to tell that story to the judge or jury is what a lawyer is hired to do. That knowledge, training, skill, and discernment is "the profession" of a lawyer.

Not everything that happens can come into evidence at a trial. Some evidence is unreliable, flawed, faulty, the product of bias or prejudice, or for some other reason untrustworthy. There are rules of evidence that keep certain evidence out and let other evidence in. A skilled lawyer who has researched and knows the rules of evidence is key to getting in the evidence you need and keeping out the evidence that is unreliable, untrustworthy, or damaging to your case.

A *passionate* lawyer is also extremely important. I have had judges tell me to calm down in court because of how passionately I advocate for my client and their cause. I simply explain to these judges that I mean no disrespect to the court, but I am unapologetically passionate about the practice of law. Some judges are uncomfortable with a dedicated and impassioned presentation of a client's case. A lawyer who treats you like "just another number" or "just another case" is not going to have the concern that is the driving force behind the initiative, dedication, and passion that it takes to win your case. If I were a client, and I have been, I would want someone fighting by my side who cared about the fight as much as I do.

The next thing that you should consider are the reviews of the attorneys you interview. Increasingly, we see opportunities to review businesses and professionals for services and products online. I do want to caution you, however, about the "standards" (or lack thereof) of these reviewing sites or reviewing services. Neither Google® nor AVVO® require reviewers to have personal relationship or experiences with the businesses they are reviewing. You really need to read between the lines of a review and see not only what's written, but what's not written. Be observant and look for biased reviews. It is possible, and I have seen it happen many times, that opposing parties, including the opposing parties' friends, family, and witnesses, will leave bad reviews for a lawyer who "beat them in court" as retaliation for losing the case.

It is possible for opposing lawyers, who are in competition with each other as legal services providers, to also leave bad reviews for their opposing lawyer or competitor. Google® and Avvo® do not actively police or regulate the truth of online reviews and the relationship of the reviewer to the business. Most people are not going to dig much further than the review itself, but you should if you want to find a competent, qualified attorney to handle their case.

Another thing to look at is the number of reviews. Some firms have a five-star rating, but they only have one review. A large number of reviews in a short period of time is also highly suspect. This can indicate that there is a lack of longevity with that law firm, or that those reviews are the result of a "solicited review campaign" sponsored by that firm. There are businesses that pay for reviews, give prizes for reviews, or even pay people to create reviews for them. Reviews can be helpful if they are true, honest, and real. However, reviews alone are not a complete indicator of a lawyer's ability. Therefore, reviews should be just one of many factors that you consider before making the decision of who to hire as your lawyer.

CHAPTER 3

WHY CHOOSE A BOARD-CERTIFIED LAWYER TO HANDLE YOUR CASE?

Within the Texas legal community, board certification means that an attorney has substantial relevant experience in a select field of law, as well as a demonstrated and tested special competence in that area of law. Board certification is a mark of excellence. I am board certified as a specialist in "Family Law" by the State Bar of Texas' Board of Legal Specialization. That title required me to pass a board certification exam after I had met a rigorous application requirement. I had to provide details about the cases I handled, including what was in dispute, the amount of property involved, and how the case was eventually ended. The application process alone is extensive, and in combination with the exam, makes becoming board certified difficult, time-consuming, and challenging. Therefore, being board certified is a high honor as a practicing attorney.

Family law cases involve all cases related to the family, such as divorce, child custody, custody modification, adoption, grandparents' access, and child support. If you are in a battle for your family, your children, or your financial future, you need an "expert." There are more than a 100,000 attorneys licensed to practice in the state of Texas, but only 858, as of 2019, were board certified in family law. That is less than one percent (1%) of all the attorneys licensed in Texas, and I am a part of that one percent (1%).

Board certified lawyers earn the right to publicly represent themselves as a "specialist" or "expert" in their specialty area of the law. They are the only attorneys allowed by the State Bar of Texas to do so. This designation sets them apart as being an attorney with the highest public commitment to excellence in their specialized area of law. The process is voluntary and can only take place after an attorney has been in practice for five years with a minimum of three years' experience in the specialty area. Moreover, board certification is not a one-time event. It requires an ongoing involvement in the specialty area, which is periodically substantiated with references from peers in that field. It also requires annual professional refreshment through the Texas Board of Legal Specialization's approved continuing legal education course work.

An attorney who is BOARD CERTIFIED in family law is an "expert" in family law. As a result, board-certified attorneys can quickly analyze a case, the legal issues involved, and advise you on the various options you may have in handling your case. Before a case goes to trial, there will be many decisions that must be made which impact your case, and consequently your life, and the lives of your children, both during and after the divorce. Many of the decisions that are made are strategic ones. Many times, a trial is like a war, which is a sustained campaign of smaller battles that ultimately decide a winner. How many times have you heard the phrase, "He won the battle but lost the war"? You don't want that to be you. You want to win, you need to win, and winning is made up of good tactical, strategic, and sound decisions based upon good intelligence and facts. Historically, many battles have been won by armies and forces of inferior numbers, but whose commanders were better strategists, better planners, better gatherers of enemy intelligence, or possessed special knowledge of the lay of the land. They won the battles *and* the wars not because of superior numbers, but because of the commander's superior knowledge and experience.

There is a story from Texas history that illustrates this point. The Battle of San Jacinto is where Texas won its independence from Mexico. General Santa Anna had a force greatly outnumbering the Texan Army, but the Texans were led by General Sam Houston, who knew the geography of San Jacinto. Houston knew that San Jacinto was a peninsula, surrounded on three sides by impassable marshes and bogs. After the Mexican Army followed the Texans onto that fateful piece of land, General Sam Houston directed Deaf Smith, his trusted scout, to burn Vince's Bridge. That bridge was the only way of escape to the mainland. General Houston then waited to attack. When the Mexican Army had stayed up all night, preparing and waiting for the Texans to attack, and the attack did not come, the Mexican Army went to sleep. At 4:30 in the afternoon, in the middle of the Mexican army's siesta, the Texan army attacked. The Mexican army was startled, disoriented, and unprepared for the strike. Within 18 minutes from when the assault started, the Mexican Army had abandoned their camp and fled for their lives into the marshes and bogs of San Jacinto. Santa Anna, the General and Supreme Ruler of Mexico, was captured in the marshy bog near the burned Vince's Bridge, and was brought to General Sam Houston. Houston watched with the rest of the Texan army as General Santa Anna surrendered his army, and his claim to Texas, thus winning Texas's independence from an army of overwhelming force, which they could not have otherwise overcome.

It was Sam Houston's expert knowledge of the land, and excellent military strategy that led to his victory over a far superior force. In the same way, having a board-certified lawyer brings an "expert," with great education and experience to work on your case. With the expert working on your side, many times you can avoid fighting over things that really don't matter or make a difference in the law, and instead spend your time and money on the legal issues that really do determine how your case turns out.

Additionally, board-certified attorneys know the law on issues affecting your case. They are equipped with legal research and other tools that can help convince the judge or jury to decide a legal issue in your favor, because the expert has extensively researched the law and is well acquainted with the latest developments as well as the historical development of the law in particular areas. Lawyers who are <u>not</u> board-certified may or may not be as up to date on the law or legal issues as a board-certified family lawyer. Therefore, they likely do not know the answers to complicated legal theories or positions without doing a large amount of "learning" the law, which your board-certified expert already has learned. Many times, I have seen lawyers who are not board-certified take the wrong position on a legal issue and spend countless hours (and consequently much of their client's money), only to lose at a hearing or trial, after a board-certified lawyer shows the judge what the current law governing that disputed legal issue. Similarly, I have seen judges, based on their own knowledge and experience of the law, point out to non-board-certified lawyers that their position on the legal issue is incorrect.

I have also observed cases where neither side's lawyer is board-certified, and those lawyers spend hours arguing over assets, debts, retirement accounts, alimony, or "fault basis" of a divorce case, neither one knowing they are both wrong on the law and its effect on the disputed issue. You may have heard the saying, "Don't bring a knife to a gun fight." When you hire a lawyer, who is not board certified, you are bringing a knife to a gun fight. A board-certified lawyer doesn't guarantee a win, but it certainly maximizes your opportunity for victory.

CHAPTER 4

WHAT AM I GOING TO DO TO GET PREPARED FOR DIVORCE?

The number one way to prepare for a divorce is to begin to gather evidence while you still have it available to you. You never want to put the judge in the position of having to take your word for anything. Almost anything you say under oath is "evidence" the judge can consider. While that is true, it is always the better practice to have documentation to back up what you say or what you observed. Documents have a way of disappearing after your spouse learns that you have filed a Petition for Divorce, or met with an attorney. For instance, many people catch their spouse cheating on them, but they don't preserve any evidence such as documents or things like videos, texts, or social media posts to prove it. Remember, "Court is not about the truth, or what really happened; it's about what you can prove."

It is a crime to destroy evidence, but in my experience, it is a crime rarely prosecuted. Judges can't make someone produce something that's been destroyed. People need to save, preserve, and protect any evidence that will back up what they know the truth to be. For instance, if you catch your spouse cheating on you by finding a photograph or video of one of their liaisons, then take a picture of that photograph, copy the photograph, and (this is the most important step) store those copies off the premises of where you live and/or work, so that the offending spouse cannot gain access to the evidence you have preserved and destroy it. Many times, I have seen people catch their spouse in a lie, infidelity, or financial impropriety, and make a copy of evidence, only to leave the copy on their electronic device at home, or in some other place to which the offending spouse has access. Later, when they need such evidence, they find it missing or destroyed. Just because you have evidence stored on your smartphone does not mean it is safe. A cell phone can be "accidently" lost, damaged, or outright destroyed by a spouse. Once you have evidence, copy it several times and store it in different locations off-site, so that your spouse or the opposition cannot find it and destroy the evidence.

Destruction of evidence is illegal, but if it is destroyed, and you have not preserved a copy of the evidence in another place, you may not be able to prove the evidence was destroyed, or that it ever existed in the first place.

You may also want to create a new email account. Be careful, to pick passwords, passphrases, and password hints, that are based upon information that your spouse does not have or does not know about you. Many times, people open new email accounts, bank accounts, or other confidential information sources, but choose a password that the other spouse knows or can figure out, based upon their knowledge of their spouse. Think and be careful!

Do not "hack" into your spouse's computer, personal cellular device, Facebook® account, or other electronically stored information, *even if you have their login credentials*. Texas is one of many states that has laws against accessing a computer or electronically stored information without the owner's consent. This area of law in Texas is still developing, so even though you are married to the person, and during happier times that person gave you the login credentials to access the cell phone, computer, or internet account (electronically-stored information), it is illegal for you to "access" electronically-stored information without the permission of the owner. This matter of evidence gathering should be discussed with your lawyer very carefully after that lawyer has done research on the current state of the law as it affects your situation. *Be careful!*

The Watergate Scandal is an excellent example of why destroying evidence is never a good idea. The Watergate Scandal, where persons broke into the headquarters of the Democratic National Committee and stole documents and secret strategy information. The men and their accomplices were caught, tried, and convicted, not only for the burglary, but also for destroying evidence and covering up the crime. President Richard Nixon, who was implicated in the plot, was forced to resign the presidency of the United States.

Another step in preparing for divorce is saving money. Many times, people will make the decision to divorce at the spur of the moment without any pre-planning, without any prior financial arrangements being made, and without having a place to go. Individuals put themselves into a desperate situation through a lack of planning. Divorce is a serious matter and should not be approached in a casual manner lightly. A wise person would recognize divorce for what it is--a life-changing event! They should put money aside, figure out where they're going to live (if they must move at all), and figure out where their kids are going to go to school *before* filing for divorce. Remember, "A failure to plan is a plan to fail!"

If you have minor children, do not leave the marital residence unless your physical safety is at risk. Even then, you should discuss the option of leaving the marital residence with your lawyer. Many judges insist that the status quo of the children not be disturbed and choosing to leave the home without your children subjects you to a strong likelihood of losing the right to establish where your children live. The parent with the right to establish where the children live is the parent/conservator who possesses what most people refer to as "having custody" of the children. The "managing conservator" has the "exclusive right" to decide where the child(ren) live and is primarily responsible for their day to day care arrangements.

Once you lose custody on a temporary basis, it sets you up to have the tough job of convincing that same judge to change their mind and give custody back to you at the final divorce hearing. It is completely possible for you to lose custody and be ordered to pay your spouse child support, even though you've been the primary caregiver since their birth. Making the decision to leave the home without the children could turn the tables on your whole custody case and turn an otherwise winning position into a losing case. However, it's not a hopeless case if you do leave the marital residence without your children. I've represented people who have left the home without the children and obtained custody in the final trial. It can be done, but if you're the primary caregiver to your children, you do not want to leave the residence that those children are used to unless your life depends on it. If you are being beaten, physically or sexually abused, or if your life is being threatened, then you are a victim of "family violence." If you are suffering family violence, you should report this to law enforcement immediately and seek protection from your abuser.

Another mistake people often make is paying down huge amounts of community debt or expenses with separate assets that belonged to them before marriage. You should not pay off any debts that are community property debts before filing for divorce. Texas is a community property state, meaning that debts made by the parties during the marriage are community debts that both spouses have a responsibility for. If you spend your money to pay down community property debts, the money is not obligated to be repaid by the other spouse who benefited from those payments. Leave the community property debts for the court to decide which of you should pay, and in what amounts.

Do not help the spouse you are about to divorce by paying down debt; you need to save money to pay for a lawyer. It takes two to agree and only one to disagree. If you are in the unfortunate position of being married to someone who wants to make a fight of your divorce, you need to have financing in place to pay for that fight. No good lawyer is going to work for free. You don't want to get a bad deal just to make a deal, because you could not afford to go to trial and fight for what was legitimately yours.

If you have access to community credit cards, consider paying your lawyer with those community credit cards. One of the exceptions to the standing restraining order that many courts in Texas have now adopted, is that a party can incur debt to pay for "reasonable and necessary attorneys' fees." If you have a large credit limit, you may even think about prepaying, into your attorney's trust account, the anticipated total costs for the divorce. The trust account proceeds remain yours and are completely refundable when the case is over, if not used. As I say, "Better to have money you don't need, than to need money you don't have." I have even had clients who will get small amounts of "cash back" at the grocery store or gas station for months and months, and use that money to pay for a lawyer.

If you have been a homemaker, or "stay at home mom," you should prepare for divorce by getting a job or figuring out a means of supporting yourself and any minor children for whom you are responsible. Warning: once you get a job, you *must* keep track of the number of hours you're working or are otherwise away from your children. Many times, people undermine their case for custody because they're trying to provide for their children by getting a job, and in so doing, they get a job that takes them away from their children more than 40 hours per week.

Therefore, the other parent has more time available to care for the children than they do.

If you have never entered the workforce, or do not have a degree or special trade, consider going back to school now, before a divorce. Yes, education is expensive, but you should not expect the court to order your spouse to support you post-divorce for a lengthy period of time, if at all. Although you can request post-divorce maintenance, as will be seen later in Chapter 12, there are no guarantees—you must be able to support yourself and your children without the help of your spouse's income.

CHAPTER 5

WHAT AM I GOING TO DO?
HOW DOES A DIVORCE CASE WORK IN TEXAS?

A divorce case begins by one party to the marriage filing an Original Petition for Divorce. When the clerk of court receives the filed petition for divorce, your divorce case is then randomly assigned to a district court or county court at law, which has been given jurisdiction (permission) to hear divorce cases. After the petition is filed, a copy of the petition is "served" by a sheriff's deputy, constable, or private process server licensed by the Supreme Court of Texas by physically handing a copy of the Original Petition for Divorce to your spouse. This copy will also have a "citation" attached to it, which gives your spouse a deadline in which to file a written answer. If your spouse files the original petition, which starts the divorce case, you must file a written answer, and in some cases, a counter-petition for divorce. If you have been served with an original petition for divorce by your spouse, you need to begin searching for an expert attorney to represent you as soon as possible! Do *not* wait until the day before your answer is due to start calling around for an attorney. Many reputable attorneys will not take cases where someone has waited until the last minute to seek legal counsel. There are unique reasons why, in some cases, a person would only file an answer and at other times file a counter-petition for divorce.

If you and your spouse have been talking about an "agreed divorce," you may be asked by your spouse or their attorney to sign a "waiver of citation". While there are different versions of this waiver of citation, great care should be exercised in deciding to sign and file such a waiver. The waiver of citation, once signed by a party to a suit and filed, allows your spouse can move forward with the suit without informing you of any other legal action he or she takes in the future. Additionally, signing and then filing this waiver of citation, in most cases, will not allow you to have any say in the terms and conditions upon which your divorce will be granted. Said another way, the "waiver of citation" is like giving your spouse a blank check. They can go into court and get divorced when they want, how they want, and get all they want, even if it is *everything*. You could be left without any assets of the marriage *and* obligated to pay all the debts of the marriage! It is at such times that you need a lawyer to assist you in evaluating your current life circumstances, and your future needs and goals, before deciding what to file on your behalf.

There are essentially two different kinds of divorce: fault or no-fault. Texas is a no-fault divorce state, meaning that if you want a divorce, you have a constitutional right to obtain a divorce without having to prove "fault" or blame on your spouse. You can simply testify, under oath, that the marriage has become "insupportable" due to a conflict of personalities that destroys the legitimate ends of the marriage relationship, and that there is no reasonable expectation of reconciliation.

A divorce can also be obtained on a "fault" basis. In such a case, the person seeking a divorce must prove that the other party has committed some "fault" in the breakup of the marriage, such as "adultery," "cruelty," "conviction of a felony offense in which the sentence is one year or more," "abandonment,"[2] "living apart[3]" or "confinement in a mental hospital[4] for three years or more."

It is usually of little legal consequence which party files first in a case where fault is alleged; although there may be some

---

[2] Meaning: that the abandoning spouse intended to abandon the other spouse and has remained away for at least one year. See, Texas Family Code, Section 6.005.

[3] For 3 or more years, Texas Family Code, Section §6.006.

[4] Texas Family Code, Section §6.007.

strategic advantages to filing first, depending on the facts of your case. After the initial divorce petition is filed, there will likely be a Standing Restraining Order issued. These Standing Restraining Orders are issued in many Texas counties when the divorce petition is first filed. The Standing Restraining Order is not necessarily issued because any person asked for one, or because of what one of the spouses has done or threatened to do. Standing Restraining Orders are increasingly being used by courts to prevent parties from committing acts the courts want to prevent, or from failing to do certain acts that courts want to continue. There may also be Temporary Restraining Orders issued by the court apart from, or in addition to, the standing restraining order. Standing Restraining Orders apply to all cases filed. They become effective the moment the divorce or child custody case is filed.

On the other hand, Temporary Restraining Orders are usually specifically requested by one or both spouses in a case and are specifically designed for stopping or preventing harm of a particular kind. A Temporary Restraining Order (TRO) is not the same thing as a "Protective Order" and does not necessarily mean that there has been any misbehavior by you or your spouse. A TRO is a series of prohibitions that require the parties to maintain the current status quo of their conduct toward each other. Parties are prohibited from destroying any property or documents that may be relevant in the divorce, changing their children's school or daycare, making any large or unusual purchases, selling any major assets, or destroying the other spouse's possessions, among other restrictions. The purpose of the TRO is to prevent one spouse from making any large changes without the consent of the other spouse.

The next step in a divorce case is a Temporary Order Hearing. This is optional, unless the other party requests Temporary Orders. Texas has no "legal separation." The closest thing Texas has which is comparable to "legal separation" in other states, is "Temporary Orders." It is possible to file for and obtain a divorce in Texas without having a temporary order hearing. However, in most cases where there is significant property or children involved, filing for Temporary Orders is advisable. In a custody case, if you and your spouse cannot agree on who should live in the marital residence, where the children should live, or what bills should be paid by each spouse, during the time that the divorce case is being made ready for presentation at a trial. A temporary orders hearing can be very helpful to preserving the status quo. In a temporary order hearing, a judge will hear from both parties, and possibly other witnesses, and hear only such evidence which is necessary to make a temporary ruling on issues of use of property, temporary child custody, and spousal and child support.

The temporary order ruling which the judge makes is not final and will only remain in place until the divorce is finalized or circumstances materially change. Many people can come to a temporary agreement without having a temporary order hearing. A growing number of Texas counties, including Montgomery and Harris counties, require divorcing parties to attend mediation before a temporary order hearing. Many times, I have seen parties to a divorce who have been summoned to court for a temporary order hearing, begin talking in the hallway or conference room about what agreements they can make on a temporary basis and end up reaching an agreement on the entire divorce case. When this happens some Texas judges will allow the parties to testify as to the terms of the agreement reached and take that testimony "under advisement." Then, when the mandatory 60-day waiting period is over, the judge may sign a Final Decree of Divorce that has been prepared in the interim, circulated and signed by the parties and their attorneys. Many times, parties who ask for and attend a temporary orders hearing get their divorce faster than people who only file for divorce and do not request temporary orders. If you are nervous about what to do and say at a temporary order hearing; you need an experienced attorney whether you are nervous or not. An experienced attorney can help prepare you for this hearing. Preparation is the key to winning your case.

The next phase of a divorce case is discovery. "Discovery" is the process where you and your attorney ask the opposing party for all information which may be relevant in deciding the issues of your case. Discovery is a very important but often annoying phase of a trial. In a contested divorce, discovery is a crucial portion of the case. In order to answer discovery, your spouse must turn over any requested documents, text conversations, pictures, or other materials which they possess or to which they have ownership. If you utilize discovery, you find out what the other side is going to use against you *before* they use it, preventing you from experiencing a trial by ambush. A smart lawyer doesn't ask a question at trial that he doesn't already know the answer to. The way the lawyer gets those answers is by doing discovery. During the discovery process, both sides can ask questions in writing, which are called interrogatories, and in person, which are called depositions. Both sides can also request documents from the other party, which are called requests for production. There is also some information that you can get from the other side just for the asking. This is called a Rule 194 Request for Disclosure. There are no objections allowed to Request for Disclosure, and the information, once requested, must be provided.

Your lawyer should work with you to prepare your documents, papers, and things, if they are requested, as well as review and explain the documents provided by your spouse.

Many times, you can discover valuable information in the discovery phase which can dramatically increase your opportunity to win at trial. The discovery phase provides you the information that allows for a "fair and equitable" division of the property acquired during the marriage (marital property). The discovery phase of a case forces parties to disclose all assets and liabilities, *if*, and it's a big if, you ask for it. If you do not spend time and money on the discovery phase, you may be unable to determine whether a settlement offer made to you is fair or equitable, because you do not know and cannot determine the total property that was available to be included in that settlement or deal. Many times, I have seen parties leave money on the table because they did not spend the time, money, and effort to conduct discovery. I find it ironic that people often file for divorce because they can no longer *trust* their spouse, and yet when it comes to the discovery phase, they take their spouse's word for what property, bank accounts, or retirement balances exist, without any kind of verification or documentation.

In one of my recent cases, where the verdict was decided by a jury, I represented a woman who had been married to an engineer in the oil industry for nineteen years. This woman only had access to the money that her husband chose to give her or deposit in the joint bank account. When the husband "cut-off" the wife financially, she was compelled to file for divorce in order to get the court to force her husband to pay the bills and expenses of the marital home. During the discovery phase of the case, I was able to obtain documentation that I used to uncover secret bank accounts that the husband maintained, which the wife was completely unaware of. This discovery information also led me to evidence that the husband had secretly diverted, with the assistance of his employer, as much as one-half of his total paycheck each pay period for many years to a secret account he had set up. Until my team found this information in discovery, my client had no idea that the husband was diverting up to one-half of his income into his secret account, which he used for his own purposes. When the jury decided this case, my client was awarded one half of all the money her husband had diverted into the secret account, and her now ex-husband was ordered to pay the wife's attorney's fees and expenses! If you and your attorney do the hard work of discovery, it can pay off dramatically.

The discovery process can be extremely complicated, and the rules governing what information you can get from the other side, and how you get it, are difficult to understand. You need an expert attorney to do this discovery for you. It is money well spent. Most lawyers hate discovery, and most judges hate discovery disputes. Although it is a difficult job and disputes may arise, discovery is often the most useful and powerful weapon in winning your case. Knowing how to get evidence is crucial to winning your case.

In my opinion, many lawyers are lazy. Despite being paid, these lawyers do not want to do the hard work of discovery. Many lawyers, when they agree to represent a person, do not charge enough money to conduct the discovery phase of the case for their client. Consequently, they do not ask for discovery, or do a poor job of it, and as a result the needed information, evidence, and proof is not obtained. Therefore, their client loses valuable assets, money, or judicial relief they could have been granted by the court, had the information been known and obtained.

Discovery is not always about money or assets. Sometimes it is about obtaining a "fault" basis for the divorce. I represented a wife whose husband suddenly left her and their minor children with no explanation. This husband was a local businessman, a deacon in his local church, and the couple had been married to his wife more than 18 years. No one knew what had caused the husband to do this. Based upon my years of experience, I suggested to the wife that it might be because the husband was committing adultery. The wife argued and argued with me about my theory. Because of the man's long held religious beliefs the wife was convinced he would not do cheat on her. We sent discovery to the husband, which included interrogatories[5]. We took the man's

[5] Interrogatories are a series of questions sent to a party or witness in a case, which must be answered in writing under oath. The person who answers, answers under penalty of perjury. Giving false testimony in Interrogatories may subject the offending party to criminal prosecution for perjury, which can be prosecuted in Texas as a felony offense.

deposition[6]. During the husband's deposition, he stated repeatedly that he was not having an affair. My client reviewed some of the documents that we received from the husband in response to our Request for Production of Documents. Taking the information in the documents provided by her husband, my client did some digging and found a phone number that she didn't recognize. She traced the suspicious phone number to an address she did not recognize, in a town a significant distance from their marital residence. I finally convinced the wife to drive down to the address and see if she could find out more information. Early one Saturday morning, as my client pulled up to the driveway of the house, the garage door opened and out walked her husband in shorts and bare feet. He picked up the newspaper and walked back into the house. A few moments later he walked out of the house hand-in-hand with another woman. They traveled to a local store, stopping in the parking lot for a kiss.

In this same case, I found during discovery that the husband had incurred credit card debt, without the wife's knowledge, totaling more than $250,000! Recall that I told you that under Texas law, a spouse can be held responsible for the repayment of debts that are incurred during the marriage. This

---

[6] Deposition is an "interview" of a party or witness in which the witness is sworn under penalty of perjury to answer truthfully. Normally, a Court Reporter makes a stenographic record of the questions and answers. Depositions may also be videotaped.

wife could have been held responsible for $250,000 in debt created secretly by her husband, because they were created on community credit cards during the marriage. Therefore, sometimes it is necessary to conduct discovery not because you have a lot of money or assets, but because it is necessary to ensure that you will not get stuck paying debt you knew nothing about and received no benefit from.

At final trial of this case, my client was granted a divorce on the grounds of adultery. The court awarded my client ownership of the family business, and ordered her husband to pay the credit card debt that was not otherwise discharged by my suit against the credit card companies. The award of the family business to my client allowed this homemaker who had not worked outside the home, but instead raised the couple's children, to have a source of income with which to support herself in the years to come. In Texas, spousal maintenance (sometimes referred to as alimony) is limited depending upon the length of marriage. However, in this case my client received much, much more money by being awarded the business than she would have ever received under a spousal maintenance award. You or your attorney may conduct discovery and never obtain such valuable information. But if you or your attorney choose not to ask for discovery, for whatever reason, you risk leaving valuable assets, money, or claims that would have dramatically changed not only the outcome, but you and your children's future livelihood.

This is also an example of why hiring a "flat fee" or "low cost" attorney is a bad idea. An attorney who does not plan on conducting discovery and therefore does not calculate that work into the flat fee or low-cost divorce price that they quote to you, will not do the hard, difficult, but necessary, work of discovery. This failure will leave you potentially spending thousands of dollars paying for debts that you knew nothing about, until it is too late to do anything about them—except pay them! Cheap is not always cheap.

The next phase of trial is mediation. Many courts require mediation as a part of the process of obtaining a divorce. Mediation is the process where a neutral third party, called a mediator, who has specialized training in resolving disputes, will help you and your spouse reach an agreement. Your attorney will be present during mediation to protect your legal interests and help you negotiate effectively. Agreements reached during the mediation process are binding and enforceable as a contract. The parties of a divorce may choose to make a mediated settlement agreement "irrevocable," which means that when the settlement is signed, neither party can change the agreement or revoke their consent to it. However, declaring your mediated settlement to be irrevocable is optional and your attorney may advise you not to agree to an irrevocable settlement. You should therefore plan to conduct discovery and take your time to make certain that you are fully aware of the all the facts and assets of your case before moving forward into the mediation phase.

The next phase is the final trial. At the final trial, all the issues and the evidence will be presented to a judge or a jury for decision. You have a choice on whether to have a bench trial, where a single judge hears your case and makes a decision, or a jury trial. In a jury trial, six or twelve citizens from your community make the ultimate decision on your case. In Texas, you are entitled to a jury trial for the most important issues of a family law case, such as which parent should have the right to establish a child's residence, or if one party is at fault for a divorce. However, there are some issues, by law, that are not able to be decided by a jury. However, the decision on which parent should have the right to establish the residence of the child is a decision that a jury is authorized to make. Whether or not a party has engaged in some "fault" in the breakup of the marriage is also a jury question.

It is important to realize that not all lawyers are trial lawyers. If your divorce case goes to trial, you will need an attorney who can help you successfully present your side of the story to a judge or jury. You need an attorney who is an accomplished public speaker, a strategist, and has a proven track record of successful court battles. I personally believe that you need an attorney who is passionate not just about your case, but about you and how you fare at the outcome of your case.

CHAPTER 6

WHAT AM I GOING TO DO? FILE FIRST?
ADVANTAGES OF FILING FIRST FOR A DIVORCE

The party who files for divorce first is usually permitted the right to present their evidence first. That party also gets to choose to close the evidence, meaning that they get the last word with the judge or the jury. Having the right to the last word in a trial may seem insignificant; but time and again, I have seen it play out to be a tremendous advantage. If you are considering divorce, and you know that your spouse is also considering a divorce, you should try to be the first to file, because having the last word can be so crucial.

There are plenty of other reasons why you should file for divorce first. In some cases, the party who files first can pick the court in which they file. Some judges are more experienced in family law cases than others, and some judges are known for disliking family law cases. If your attorney is not very aware of the judge and each different judge's particular preferences, and your divorce case is filed in a court that dislikes family law cases, you may have additional complications in your case that could have been otherwise avoided. Filing in the correct court is important because, with a few exceptions, the judge you start with is the judge who decides your case. If your case is unfortunately filed in a court having preferences, biases, or prejudices, you and your lawyer will have more difficulty convincing a judge to rule in your favor. Additionally, judges have the right to regulate the amount of time a case is given, which means that your court time may be limited by a judge who dislikes family law. If you file first, an experienced attorney will know which courts to avoid for your specific kind of case.

The party who files for divorce will pay the initial filing fees, which are typically slightly higher than those of a counter petition or responsive pleading. If you are sued for divorce or any other type of action as a respondent or a defendant, you can file a counterclaim. The decision to initiate a divorce or custody case should be thoroughly discussed with your attorney. Standing restraining orders typically prohibit changing a child's residence.

Therefore, if your child's primary residence is with you at the time of filing, that residency will typically remain unchanged for the purposes of a divorce or custody suit. If your spouse is or is likely to be harassing you, hiding or changing bank accounts, your attorney can ask the court for a temporary restraining order, discussed earlier on Page 48. A TRO is different from the "standing restraining order," discussed earlier on page 41. Your lawyer can put whatever terms they want in the request for a restraining order and if the judge approves it, your spouse would then be prohibited by court order from doing one or more of the bad acts prohibited by the TRO.

There is a certain degree of strategy involved in filing the initial divorce or child custody suit that should be discussed and planned out with the lawyer you have chosen to represent you. Only by filing for Divorce, Suit To Affect The Parent Child Relationship, Paternity, or Termination and Adoption can you get court orders for possession, access, or support of a child. If you are married, have entered an Order Determining Paternity, or have filed an Acknowledgement of Paternity form with the Texas Bureau of Vital Statistics, then both parents have equal rights to seek custody and possession of the child. If parents cannot agree on which of them will have possession of their child, a court can make orders that decide where the child is going to live while the case is progressing through the court system. A court can also prohibit a parent from "snatching" and "hiding" a child from the other parent. This is discussed more fully in the next chapter.

CHAPTER 7

HOW ARE CHILD CUSTODY ISSUES HANDLED IN A DIVORCE?

Any child born to a married couple is presumed to be, under Texas law, a child of that marriage, even if the child is not biologically related to both parents. If parents of a child separate and file for divorce, a "Suit To Affect The Parent Child Relationship" is usually joined with the divorce suit. The judge will determine parental rights and duties of each parent, custody of the child, possession rights to the child, child support, and medical support for the child. If a child's parents are not married and then separate or are already separated, and no Acknowledgement of Paternity form has been filed, then a paternity suit must be filed. A paternity suit determines the father of the child and serves to officially exclude the child from being part of a marriage in which either parent is a party.

The chief concern of those individuals who have children and are undergoing a divorce is what will happen to their children during and after the divorce. Part of the job of the judge in any divorce case involving children is to determine which parent will be charged with the duty of da-to-day care, custody, and control of the child. Many times, parents will agree amongst themselves on which of them will be the parent primarily responsible for making decisions affecting the child. If the parties cannot agree on this point, the court will make the decision. Most courts try to be extremely fair in making this determination because of "presumptions" and "state policies" under Texas law.

The parent chosen by the judge or jury is called a Managing Conservator and is awarded the right to determine the domicile[7] (residence) of the child among other rights and duties of a parent. This is often what people mean when they refer to having "custody." There are essentially two different kinds of custody in Texas: 1) Joint Managing Conservatorship, and 2) Sole Managing Conservatorship. If a conservator is a natural parent of the child, then there is a presumption under Texas law that this natural parent *shall* be named a Joint

[7] See, Texas Family Code, Section §153.132.

Managing Conservator (JMC) with the other parent of the child. However, between these two parents who are named Joint Managing Conservators, one of these JMC's must be awarded the right to establish the domicile (residence) of the child unless both JMC's agree that neither party shall have that right. In that event, one of the parties is appointed the "Joint Managing Conservator with the right to establish the domicile of the child" and that appointed person is called a Managing Conservator[8] (commonly referred to as the Custodial parent), even though in the same Divorce Decree or court order they are also called a Joint Managing Conservator. All of this can get very complicated and very confusing, very fast. I have encountered many lawyers who do not understand the significance of these different terms, even though they are lawyers. Many lawyers mistakenly use these terms interchangeably and improperly. Therefore, these differences and distinctions should be discussed with an expert family law attorney early in your case, or, ideally, before the divorce is filed. As will be discussed

---

[8] See Texas Family Code, Section §153.005.(2), which says, "if the parents are or will be separated, shall appoint at least one managing conservator." Therefore, the term "Joint Managing Conservator" is used in the Divorce Decree to describe both parents, while in the same Divorce Decree, at other points, the terms "Managing Conservator" and "Possessory Conservator" are used to distinguish which parent has the right to establish the domicile or residence of the child and other parental duties, if any, which are exclusive to that same parent. The parent with the right to establish the domicile or residence of the child is often referred to as the parent having "custody", i.e., the "Custodial" parent.

further in this chapter, you may not have equal rights and duties with the other parent or equal possession of your child even though you are a JMC along with the child's other parent.

The first kind of "custody" is "Joint Managing Conservatorship." This is the most common type of custody awarded in Texas, because there is a presumption under Texas law that natural parents of children be named a Joint Managing Conservator of their children. Parents in Texas have certain legal rights some of which are:

(a) A parent of a child has the following rights and duties:

(1) the right to have physical possession, to direct the moral and religious training, and to designate the residence of the child;

(2) the duty of care, control, protection, and reasonable discipline of the child;

(3) the duty to support the child, including providing the child with clothing, food, shelter, medical and dental care, and education;

(4) the duty, except when a guardian of the child's estate has been appointed, to manage the estate of the child, including the right as an agent of the child to act in relation to the child's estate if the child's action is required by a state, the United States, or a foreign government;

(5) except as provided by Section 264.0111, the right to the services and earnings of the child;

(6) the right to consent to the child's marriage, enlistment in the armed forces of the United States, medical and dental care, and psychiatric, psychological, and surgical treatment;

(7) the right to represent the child in legal action and to make other decisions of substantial legal significance concerning the child;

(8) the right to receive and give receipt for payments for the support of the child and to hold or disburse funds for the benefit of the child;

(9) the right to inherit from and through the child;

(10) the right to make decisions concerning the child's education; and

(11) any other right or duty existing between a parent and child by virtue of law.

(b) The duty of a parent to support his or her child exists while the child is an unemancipated minor and continues as long as the child is fully enrolled in a secondary school in a program leading toward a high school diploma and complies with attendance requirements described by Section 154.002(a)(2).

(c) A parent who fails to discharge the duty of support is liable to a person who provides necessaries to those to whom support is owed.

(d) The rights and duties of a parent are subject to:

(1) a court order affecting the rights and duties;

(2) an affidavit of relinquishment of parental rights; and

(3) an affidavit by the parent designating another person or agency to act as managing conservator.

(e) Only the following persons may use corporal punishment for the reasonable discipline of a child:

(1) a parent or grandparent of the child;

(2) a stepparent of the child who has the duty of control and reasonable discipline of the child; and

(3) an individual who is a guardian of the child and who has the duty of control and reasonable discipline of the child. The law[9] requires courts rendering an order appointing joint managing conservators to:

(1) designate the conservator who has the exclusive right to determine the primary residence of the child and:

(A) establish, until modified by further order, a geographic area within which the conservator shall maintain the child's primary residence; or

[9] See, Texas Family Code, Section §153.134.(b)

(B) specify that the conservator may determine the child's primary residence without regard to geographic location;

(2) specify the rights and duties of each parent regarding the child's physical care, support, and education;

(3) include provisions to minimize disruption of the child's education, daily routine, and association with friends;

(4) allocate between the parents, independently, jointly, or exclusively all of the remaining rights and duties of a parent as provided by Chapter 151; and

(5) if feasible, recommend that the parties use an alternative dispute resolution method before requesting enforcement or modification of the terms and conditions of the joint conservatorship through litigation, except in an emergency.

A Joint Managing Conservatorship does not mean that each parent has possession of their child 50% of the time. In a Joint Managing Conservatorship, each of the two natural parents or conservators share the above rights and duties. These rights and duties can be shared: 1) *jointly,* subject to the agreement of the other parent or conservator; 2) *independently,* meaning each parent or conservator can exercise the rights independently without obtaining consent or permission from the other parent or conservator; or 3) All of the available rights are awarded to one parent or conservator *exclusively*. As you can see, just because you are named a Joint Managing Conservator does not mean you have equal rights with the other parent. This is another reason why you need an attorney to represent you in your divorce or custody suit. A devious opposing party or their attorney can write a custody order giving one side all the significant rights regarding the child, even though it is called by name a Joint Managing Conservatorship. Said another way, just because it says *Joint* does not necessarily mean it is *joint* in reality.

The second kind of custody is "Sole Managing Conservatorship." A Sole Managing Conservator normally has all the rights and duties of a parent *exclusively*, save and except the obligation to pay child support. Unless limited by court order, a parent appointed as sole managing conservator of a child has the following exclusive rights[10]:

(1) the right to designate the primary residence of the child;

(2) the right to consent to medical, dental, and surgical treatment involving invasive procedures;

(3) the right to consent to psychiatric and psychological treatment;

(4) the right to receive and give receipt for periodic payments for the support of the child and to hold or disburse these funds for the benefit of the child;

---

[10] See, Texas Family Code, Sec. §153.132.

(5) the right to represent the child in legal action and to make other decisions of substantial legal significance concerning the child;

(6) the right to consent to marriage and to enlistment in the armed forces of the United States;

(7) the right to make decisions concerning the child's education;

(8) the right to the services and earnings of the child;

(9) except when a guardian of the child's estate or a guardian or attorney ad litem has been appointed for the child, the right to act as an agent of the child in relation to the child's estate if the child's action is required by a state, the United States, or a foreign government;

(10) the right to

(A) apply for a passport for the child;

(B) renew the child's passport; and

(C) maintain possession of the child's passport.

The parent not awarded the right to determine the domicile of the child is usually called the "Possessory Conservator." The Possessory Conservator (non-custodial parent) also is awarded certain rights and responsibilities by the judge by virtue of being a parent of the child. Texas has an official state policy which promotes frequent access and involvement in the child-rearing functions regardless of which parent is named the "custodial parent" or has "Managing

Conservatorship" (custody) of the child. Therefore, just because a parent does not have possession of the child for the majority of time it does not automatically mean that such a parent has no custody, no rights, or no say in how the child is raised.

As I said earlier, if the divorcing parties are the natural parents of the child, or adoptive parents to the child, then there is a presumption under Texas law that the parents should be named Joint Managing Conservators of the child. In such a case, one of those JMC would typically be awarded the right to establish the residence, or domicile, of the child. It is this right which determines, in most people's minds, which of the two parents has full custody. However, refer to the previous pages in this chapter and specifically to footnote number 7 to see the confusion that often occurs with the different titles and terminology, used when the Final Decree or Order in Suit to Affect Parent-Child Relationship is prepared.

The determination by the judge or jury of which parent should be the Managing Conservator and which parent should be the Possessory Conservator, is based on what is in "the best interest of the child." A parent's lawyer will each present that parent's parenting plan or reasons why that parent should be awarded primary[11] custody of the child and will present

---

[11] "Primary" is a word often used to distinguish between Joint Managing Conservators: which of the Joint Managing Conservators has the right to establish the residence of the child. As explained earlier in this book,

evidence of which parent is best suited to provide for the child's physical and emotional needs, provide a stable and safe home environment, ensure educational progress and development, and foster good relationships between the other parent, extended family, and the child. The judge or jury also have several other factors they use in determining a Managing Conservator based upon the best interest of the child standard.

Once the court has determined which parent the child will primarily reside with, the next question most people have is "What amount of time will the other parent have with the child?" Texas has a "Standard Possession Order" (SPO) that specifies the "minimum" amount of possession ("visitation," as it is often referred to) that a non-custodial parent will have with their child. The Standard Possession Order is probably what you are most familiar with. The SPO is basically, 1st, 3rd, and 5th weekends of each month, and every Thursday during the school term, plus some portion of holidays, and spring break.[12]

Managing Conservatorship is this right to establish the domicile of the child. This is the chief right of the Conservatorship, which the law says distinguishes which parent has more rights regarding the child than the other parent. It is the tug of war of this distinctive right which sets up a lot of the winner versus loser notions which prompted the Texas Legislature to make changes to the Texas Family Code allowing parents to "agree to disagree" about the right to establish the domicile of the child, by agreeing to award this right to either parent of the child. See, Texas Family Code, Section §153.133.(c)(2).

12 See Texas Fam. Code, Section 153.312-317. This includes the different alternatives for possession of a child by the possessory conservator, depending on various elections and distance between the child's residence and the possessory conservator's residence.

However, the Standard Possession Order (SPO) **does not apply to children under age 3**. Although the "Standard Possession Order" (SPO) is the "minimum" amount of time a parent may be awarded by a Court, many parents think this is all the possession of their child that they can get or are entitled receive. This is not necessarily the case, as parents can agree on additional times of possession and access to their children. There are "elections" a non-custodial parent can make to gain even more time with their child. The elections, once made, can come very close to a near 50/50 split of parenting time with your child.

Divorcing parents may reach a mutual agreement to allow one parent additional time with the child beyond the original court order. A word of caution: once a court order for possession and access is signed by the judge, it would be prudent for all agreements between parents for additional time of possession by the non-custodial parent to be reduced to a single writing, signed, and dated by both parties. These agreements should contain terms specifying the date and time for pickup, and re-deliver date and time, which has been agreed to by the parties. The reason for this is that sometimes miscommunication occurs. If the agreement is in a single writing (not an email chain) signed and dated by the parents, there is less opportunity for miscommunication. Any time a Conservator (person with court-ordered rights to a child) has possession of the child outside the times and dates written in the possession order signed by the judge, that person is open to an accusation that they are in unlawful possession of the child. In a worst case scenario such a parent could be charged with "parental kidnapping" or some other violation of the criminal law, as well as, or in addition to, a civil violation of a Court Order, which could carry a conviction for contempt of court, fines, risking court costs and payment of the opposition's attorney fees. It simply is not worth the risk. The better practice is to put any departures from the court's written order in writing and have that writing signed and dated by both parties.

In extreme cases, a judge may decide that a parent should *not* be allowed possession or access to their child at all. Judges may also award more, or even less, time to a parent than the SPO provides for so long as the judge makes a judicial "finding" that the departure from the SPO "is in the child's best interest" or that to award a parent/party the SPO "would NOT be in the child's best interest."

As stated earlier, the "Standard Possession Order"[13] is a Court Order which specifies the ***minimum*** amount of possession (visitation) that a Possessory Conservator (the parent who does not have primary custody) shall have with the child. The SPO

---

[13] The "Standard Possession Order" can be found in the Texas Family Code, at: Section §153.3101.-§153.317.

provides conservators (parents) who reside 100 miles or less from each other a possession (visitation) schedule of generally:

a. Every first, third and fifth weekend of the month;

b. Every Thursday (during the school term only);

c. 30 continuous days[14] during the summer;

d. Alternating holidays.

The "standard possession order" specifies the beginning and ending time for all periods of possession to be 6:00 p.m. on Fridays of a possession period, and ending the following Sunday at 6:00 p.m. In some cases, the beginning and ending time of possession periods may be at the time the child is released from school and when school resumes after a weekend.

It is the Friday of the weekend which determines if that particular weekend is a first, third, or fifth weekend for possession purposes. It does not matter if the entire weekend is completely contained in that same month or continues into the next month. In some cases, a parent may choose or "elect" an *expanded* period of possession of their child that begins when that child is released from school until the beginning of the next school day following that period of possession began. If the

---

[14] "Continuous" meaning day to day for a period of 30 days. However, the custodial parent may "interrupt" this 30 day period on a designated weekend during this 30 day period, provided that the parent who is interrupting, must travel to where ever the Possessory Conservator is with the child and pick up the child from the Possessory Conservator at that place and must return the child at the conclusion of that weekend visit to the Possessory Conservator at that same place. See, Texas Family Code., Section §153.312.(b)(3).

Possessory Conservator makes this choice or "election," they are also entitled to overnight possession of the child on *every* Thursday during the regular school term. As you can see, this can quickly add up to a significant amount of time for the Possessory Conservator; it is almost a 50/50 split. Whether or not you can or should elect an "expanded possession schedule" for your child should be discussed with your attorney.

The Standard Possession Order also has "long distance" provisions for parents/conservators who live more than 100 miles apart. Under these provisions a Possessory Conservator is entitled, at a minimum, to receive:

a. First, third, and fifth weekends of each month for a period of possession of their child; or that conservator may elect an alternative possession schedule of a specified one weekend per month in which to have possession of their child;
b. 42 days in the summer for extended summer possession of the child. However, the Managing Conservator is awarded 2 weekends (instead of the 1 weekend available for parents residing under 100 miles apart) during this 42-day period when that Managing Conservator may travel to where the child is and interrupt the Possessory Conservator's period of possession, for a visit with the child, provided that the Managing Conservator pick up the child wherever the child is and return the child to that same place.

c. You will notice that there are *no* Thursday night periods of possession of the child in this "over 100 miles" possession provision.

Texas law does not require the court to award equal possession of a child to parents. [15] Some parents attempt, for various reasons, to agree to a 50/50 split of time with their children. Although this is many times a well-intentioned attempt to "not fight over custody" it is difficult to actually carry out, and *extremely* difficult to enforce with the power of the courts, because it is extremely difficult to draft an "enforceable order."

An enforceable order is a Divorce Decree or some other court order that is written in such a clear and unambiguous manner that it can be clearly understood what was ordered. Many Orders are "unenforceable" because they are poorly worded, drafted, or contain words or phrases that could mean several different things. A person may not be held in contempt of court or required to obey any order that is unclear, ambiguous, or capable of several different interpretations.

Unfortunately, sometimes the agreement of a 50/50 split of the children is not "well intentioned" at all. Instead, it is a devious attempt by one parent to avoid paying child support to the other parent. However, just because parties agree to equal possession of the child, the agreement does not prevent the

---

[15] Texas Family Code, Section §153.135.

judge from ordering one of these parents to pay child support to another parent or party.[16]

It is very important to understand that the payment or non-payment of child support is not connected in any way to possession and access of the child. Under Texas law a parent may not withhold possession of a child to another parent who is delinquent, or behind, in their child support.[17] Similarly, a parent who is denied possession of their child may not unilaterally stop or refuse to pay child support for a child that they are not being permitted to possess or visit in accordance with a valid court order.

Many times, when a parent does not pay child support the other parent will refuse to allow visitation between the child and the parent who has failed to pay child support. Parents who engage in these types of "self-help" measures in order to "solve" problems regarding payment of child support and possession often make matters worse. "Two wrongs don't make a right" and each of the parents in the above illustration are in danger of being held in contempt of court, which carries a fine of $500 and a term of up to 180 days in jail, *for each missed payment or missed visit.*

---

[16] Texas Family Code, Section §153.138., says "The appointment of joint managing Conservators does not impair or limit the authority of the court to order a joint managing Conservator to pay child support to another joint managing Conservator."

[17] Texas Family Code, Section §154.011.

CHAPTER 8
WHAT AM I GOING TO DO ABOUT CHILD CUSTODY IF I AM NOT MARRIED?

Every divorce between spouses who have parented children requires a custody suit to be joined with the divorce suit. This means that there are actually two suits in one; 1) a divorce which legally terminates the marriage and divides the marital property, and 2) A Suit To Affect Parent-Child Relationship (SAPCR). In cases where the parents were never married but need the court to make orders for custody, possession and child support, a Suit To Affect Parent-Child Relationship must be filed.

Parents who are not married but have signed an "Acknowledgment of Paternity" (AOP) form and filed it with the Texas Bureau of Vital Statistics will also need to file a SAPCR suit, to have rights and duties determined. If paternity has not been determined by an AOP, or other court action, then a "Suit to Establish the Parent-Child Relationship" (also referred to as a "paternity suit") must be filed to have the father of the child officially determined and each parent's respective rights and duties to that child specified.

A SAPCR suit necessarily involves people who are parents either because they are married or have signed a government form called an *Acknowledgement of Paternity*, or there has been a suit filed previously which established paternity. SAPCR suits may also be filed by the State of Texas, certain relatives, or any person who has had physical possession of the child or with whom a child and a parent have resided for at least 6 months, ending not more than 90 days before the suit is filed. Many parents who have physical custody of their children unwittingly place themselves and their children in the position of a contested custody battle with people who the parent thought were there to help them. However, because the assistance provided to a parent lasted for 6 months or longer, the person providing the help or support now has the lawful right to seek conservatorship of the child.

My 26 years of experience have shown me many cases where a parent inadvertently provides another person with the right to seek custody of a child. This is especially common with women, who often move in with relatives or a boyfriend during the separation associated with a divorce. If you move in with a family member or friend for more than 6 months, you will be providing the legal grounds for that person to seek full custody of your child. Be careful! If you must seek assistance or living arrangements from friends or family, try to get on your feet quickly. However, be aware that simply moving so that you do not stay longer than 6 months in any one place could send the wrong message to a judge or jury. Evidence of frequent moving can be used against you in a custody battle. Providing a "stable and safe environment" for the child is one of the factors a judge may use in determining custody of the child using the "the best interest of the child" legal standard.

Another issue involving child custody cases joined to a divorce case are what we lawyers call "move away" or "relocation" cases. Relocation cases involve situations in which one parent or conservator of the child decides to move away from the other parent or conservator. Many times, the move causes increased expenses to be incurred by the other parent to accommodate visitation (possession) rights to the child. Typically, these cases involve the desire to relocate a significant distance away from the current, established residence of the child. Relocation cases are usually very contested and are dependent upon the unique facts of each case. As a result, there has been a specialized body of law developed regarding which factors a judge or jury must consider in deciding these relocation cases. If you are involved in a relocation case, you should work very closely with your attorney to develop a strategy that deals with these factors upon which relocation cases are to be decided. You will need an experienced lawyer to guide you through the nuances of this area of the law.

In Texas, there are many factors in a child custody case which must be considered by a judge, in accordance with the Family Code. Judges are required to make their decision based upon "the best interest of the child." There has developed in current case law precedent which has determined what "the best interest of the child" is. In Texas, all child custody, possession, and child support decisions must be based off this established "best interest" standard. Judges are required to make their decision based upon that law. These best interest factors usually include an examination at trial of the relationship the child has with each parent as well as with their siblings and extended family members.

In Texas, the wishes of the child are to be considered if the child is old enough to make his or her desires known. However, these wishes are still subject to the "best interests of the child" standard. A child aged 12 or older is entitled to an interview with the judge, where the child can speak for themselves about their choice for which parent has managing conservatorship. If the child is under age 12, the child may request the interview with the judge, but cannot demand it. If the judge decides to interview a child in response to a parent's lawful request, the judge will direct the parties, through their lawyers, on the procedure for conducting that interview. Even after that interview, the judge is not required to grant the child their request. The older the child is, the more weight the courts usually give to the expressed wishes of the child. *Do not bring your child to court unless you are told to do so.* Keep the child in school until the judge or your attorney directs you to do otherwise. Having a child testify in open court in a dispute between parents is highly disfavored by most judges and juries.

There are many factors that the courts may consider when determining custody in a case. For example, each parent's mental and physical health will be assessed, as well as the environment which each parent would provide for the child to live in. If either parent has a history of abuse or neglect, of a child, this will also be considered. The degree of parental conflict or violence is also considered. The level of cooperation parents have, or don't have, with each other can be a major factor in the types of rights and duties a parent is awarded by the judge.

The school district and the local community will be considered. If you live in a high crime area or if the local school has a low rating by the Texas Education Agency, these are factors a judge can consider in making the decision on which parent should be named the conservator. Lifestyle issues that might interfere with the ability to provide a solid and stable home life for the child are considered, including the impact of cohabitation with a new partner, roommate, or other person who has frequent contact with a child.

Things such as religion may also be considered by the judge when making the decision of conservatorship. A judge cannot make a custody determination based on religion. However, if the child has an expressed and long-standing involvement in a church or religious institution, I have seen that educational, social, and societal impact in the child's life considered by judges and child custody evaluators.

Although Texans have the right to a jury determination of which parent should have custody, it is only the judge who can assign particular parental rights and duties to one parent or the other, regardless of the jury's determination. If you want to get or keep custody of your child, you will have to convince the judge or jury that it is in your child's best interest to live with you. This is especially true if you wish to obtain sole custody. You will need to present witnesses who can testify to the judge regarding the factors that are considered when determining custody. Anyone who can testify on your behalf is important to making your case and convincing the judge to decide to give you managing conservatorship of your child.

The Texas Family Code sets forth the following factors which courts are required to consider[18] in making a child custody determination are:

(1) the age, developmental status, circumstances, needs, and best interest of the child

(2) the circumstances of the Managing Conservator and of the parent named as a Possessory Conservator; and

(3) any other relevant factor.

As you can see, anything is up for consideration by a judge when the law says the judge may consider "any other relevant factor", that is a hole big enough to drive an 18-wheeler truck through.

In Texas, the "best interests of the child" is the controlling standard for making child custody, possession, and support decisions. Just because a judge is a judge, they cannot do whatever they want. Judges are required to make their decision based upon the evidence presented and the controlling standard of "the best interest of the child." The goal of most judges and the stated public policy of the State of Texas is to

---

[18] See, Texas Family Code, Section §153.256.

provide the greatest stability and the best environment for the child. These "best interest" factors[19] may and usually include:

(1) The relationship the child has with each parent, as well as with siblings and extended family members.
(2) The wishes of the child, if the child is old enough to make his or her desires known, can also be considered by a judge or jury in making a child custody decision. *Be careful not to discuss your divorce case with your child.* A parent who discusses the case (your divorce) with the child will irritate the court and, in some cases, the wrath of the judge. There is an abundance of psychological and sociological data to show that this type of activity is harmful to children.
(3) Any history of abuse or neglect on the part of either parent
(4) Each parent's mental and physical health
(5) The living environment the parent can provide to the child, including the school and local community can be considered. If you live in a high crime rate area, or if the local school has a low rating by the Texas Education Agency, then these are factors a judge can consider in making the decision on which parent should be named the Conservator with the right to establish the residence of the child.
(6) Lifestyle issues that might interfere with the ability of a parent to provide a solid and stable home life for the child

[19] See, Texas Family Code, Section §263.307.

are considered, including the impact of cohabitation with a new partner, roommate, or other person who has frequent contact with the child.

(7) Things such as religious training and education and hours worked may also be considered by the Judge in making the decision of Managing Conservatorship (custody);

(8) The degree of conflict, violence, or cooperation between the parents or conservators of the child can be a major factor of consideration in the types of rights and duties a parent is awarded by the judge in making a custody determination. The willingness (or lack thereof) of the parents to cooperate with the other party in child-rearing decisions, and to encourage a continued and "positive" relationship with the other parent for the child, are significant factors which courts consider in making a custody decision. If a parent is making attempts to influence or create bias or to "poison the child" against the other parent (sometimes called "parental alienation"), this will reflect poorly on the parent engaging in such conduct and it can seriously impact a judge's child custody decision;

(9) The ability of each parent to provide financial support for the child, including any history of missed child support and/or medical support payments or reimbursements is also a factor considered in determining "the best interest of the child."

These and other factors may be considered by the judge to determine "the best interests of the child," and consequently where the child should live, or how child possession and access to the child should be divided among the parents or conservators.

As discussed above, if you want to get or keep custody of your child, you will have to convince the judge that it is "in your child's best interests" to live with you. This is especially true if you wish to obtain "sole custody." But how do you show it is in the "best interests" of your child to live with you? This process will include some or all the following steps:

1. You will need to present witnesses that can testify to the judge regarding the above listed factors that are considered when determining custody. Contacting other family members, neighbors, teachers, and anyone else who can testify on your behalf is important to making your case and convincing the judge to decide to give you Managing Conservatorship (custody) of your child.
2. An Amicus Attorney or Attorney Ad Litem is also appointed in many custody cases to make a recommendation to the court. The Attorney Ad Litem *represents the child* in the custody dispute *and* has the *legal duty* to advocate for the *expressed wishes of the child,* without regard to whether or not those expressed wishes are in the child's own best interests.

3. The role of an Amicus Attorney is *very different,* but also similar. An Amicus attorney has two legal duties: 1) *advise* the Court of the expressed wishes of the child; 2) express to the Court what "is in the child's best interests" *regarding* the child's expressed wishes, as to the child's chosen Conservator, and the other factors described above. The Amicus attorney is authorized by a court order and may observe you, your family members, and your child to determine what the proper choice for custody is. It is imperative you cooperate with the Amicus Attorney and provide him or her with the details they need to make an informed choice on what is best for your child.

An alternative or addition to the appointment of an Attorney Ad Litem, or Amicus Attorney, is the appointment of a Custody Evaluator. The Custody Evaluations can only be performed by qualified professionals who have completed certain levels of education and training and who have been approved by the judge of the case to perform custody evaluations. A custody evaluator owes no legal obligation to the child but, as a person with a special professional and legal qualification, renders an opinion for the court on which party should receive custody.

The custody evaluator's report is subject to the Texas Rules of Evidence, which means that "hearsay" statements and other information often contained in the report may violate the Texas Rules of Evidence and make the report inadmissible into evidence at any trial. This may prevent the judge from ever reading the custody evaluation. If the custody evaluation report is inadmissible, the judge may never see the results of the report, which could be harmful or beneficial to your case, depending on the circumstances of your particular situation. For strategic reasons, great care, thought, and discussion with your lawyer should be given to the decision of whether to ask for a custody evaluation. The court will very often follow the recommendation of the custody evaluator, if that recommendation is allowed into evidence.

Remember that any evaluator, the jury, and the judge are listening to what you say, to determine what is in the best interests of your child. Sometimes what you do *not* say can significantly impact the judge's decision. If you pay too much attention to the amount of child support or are seeking custody of your child in an effort to avoid paying child support, the judge may interpret this as a lack of concern for your "child's best interests" and you may very well end up with less time with your child. Although, under Texas Law, issues of child support and custody are not connected, an evaluator, judge, or jury may confuse your over-attention to or fixation upon financial matters as an indication that it's all about the money with you, and that you are not motivated by your "child's best interest." Remember, the parent who appears most reasonable, well-adjusted, disciplined, and who can provide the safest, most stable and nurturing environment will usually win a custody battle.

To obtain Managing Conservatorship of a child you also must refrain from any behavior that could adversely impact "the best interest of the child." Do not badmouth the other parent, or interfere with the child's relationship with that parent, as these things will reflect badly on you during a custody dispute.

CHAPTER 9

WHAT AM I GOING TO DO ABOUT MY CHILD'S DIVORCE?

Grandparents are often overlooked by parents and the parents' attorneys in a divorce case. However, in Texas, grandparents have statutory rights regarding access to their grandchildren, and therefore are "potential parties" to any divorce case involving their grandchildren's parents. Unfortunately, disagreements between grandparents and their children, or disagreements between the two parents of a child, can prevent grandparents from having possession or even access to their grandchildren. Increasingly, in my practice, I see more and more grandparents being compelled to step in and raise and/or care for their grandchildren because the parents will not or cannot. In 2016,

The Public Broadcasting Service (PBS) reported[20] that "Nationwide, 2.7 million grandparents are raising grandchildren, and about one-fifth of those have incomes that fall below the poverty line, according to census figures. Their ranks are increasing. The number of grandparents raising grandchildren is up 7 percent from 2009. Experts say the trend is likely to continue as the nation responds to the opioid epidemic. Military deployment and a growth in the number of women incarcerated are other factors forcing grandparents to step into parental roles." In 2017, the U.S. Census Bureau reported that "the percentage of children living in a grandparent-headed household increased from 3 percent in 1970 to 6 percent in 2012 (Ellis and Simmons 2014). In 2016, there were 7.2 million grandparents living with their grandchildren, and over 2.5 million were responsible for their grandchildren's basic needs."

However, in Texas, grandparents have limited rights to possession and access to grandchildren. Even if you, as a grandparent, have been deeply involved in the life of your grandchild, you may not be allowed to continue that involvement

---

20 PBS NEWSHOUR, Broadcast February 16, 2016. See also, "The percentage of children living in a grandparent-headed household increased from 3 percent in 1970 to 6 percent in 2012 (Ellis and Simmons 2014). In 2016, there were 7.2 million grandparents living with their grandchildren, and over 2.5 million were responsible for their grandchildren's basic needs (US Census Bureau 2017); The Opioid Prescribing Rate and Grandparents Raising Grandchildren: State and County Level Analysis; Lydia Anderson, Presented at the Annual Meeting of the Population Association of America Austin, Texas April 10-13, 2019.

after the child's parents divorce. If you are not allowed, for whatever reason, to continue your involvement in your grandchild's life, there are limited things you can do under Texas law.

Texas has a grandparent's access statute[21]. Grandparents, depending on the circumstances, can file several different kinds of suits in order to obtain or maintain access to their grandchildren. One type of suit is called a "Suit for Grandparent's Access." Texas is one of several states that has a specific law which allows grandparents to have "access" to their grandchildren. For a grandparent to gain Court-ordered access to their grandchild, a grandparent must prove, among other things, that denial to the grandparent of possession or access to their grandchild would "significantly impair" their grandchild's "physical health or emotional well-being." This is a very difficult standard to meet. Even if a grandparent wins such "access," it is only "access," not custody. Access has been interpreted by some Texas judges to mean only telephone calls, while other judges have also awarded to grandparents regular weekend possession.

"Grandparent's Access" should not be confused with grandparents seeking custody or Managing Conservatorship of their grandchildren. Although both suits involve grandparents, they involve very different legal theories and, if a grandparent wins, different results. As stated earlier, "access" by a grandparent

---

[21] See, Texas Family Code, Section §153.432.

can be as little as phone conversations or weekend possession of a grandchild. What amount of access to award to the grandparent is completely within the opinion of the judge. There are no legislative guidelines the judge is required to follow.

If the circumstances are right, it is possible for a grandparent to be named a Sole Managing Conservator or a Joint Managing Conservator of their grandchild, instead of the natural parents of the child. A grandparent who petitions a court for custody or visitation must meet two legal requirements to gain Conservatorship (custody). First, the grandparent must establish what is called "standing." Second, the grandparent must prove that the change in custody is in "the child's best interest." In some cases, a grandparent must prove a third factor: that it is ***not*** in the grandchild's best interest that the grandchild's parents be given or retain custody.

In what situations will a grandparent have standing (the legal right) to file suit? The Texas Family Code provides several ways for grandparents to establish "standing." Of these several different ways, there are primarily two that are most often used. The first way is the "general standing." This avenue is usually for grandparents who want custody of their grandchildren. This reason is most often used in cases where a grandparent has "actual possession" of their grandchild for the last six months or more, or has primarily raised their grandchild, provided the suit is filed while the grandparent is in possession of the child or before the 90th day after the child has left the grandparents possession.

The second way is to establish a "significant impairment." A grandparent or other blood relative (within the third degree of consanguinity[22]) can file a custody suit. If a grandparent can prove to the court that the child's "present circumstances" would "significantly impair" the child's physical health, emotional or psychological development, they have established a "significant impairment." In other words, the grandparents' responsibility to prove that the child's parents are "unfit."

You may be asking, why are the laws so restrictive on grandparents? Is this just a Texas thing? No. On June 5, 2000; more than 19 years ago, the United States Supreme Court made its decision in a case called *Troxel v. Granville*. The Court reaffirmed that parents have a Constitutional right to raise their children as the please without the interference of the state, except in extraordinary circumstances. Following this ruling, many states, including Texas, were forced to amend their grandparents' statutes or at least tailor their laws' application to comply with the Supreme Court's decision in

---

[22] Third Degree of Consanguinity- Examples: Child to father is a relation one degree of consanguinity apart. Child to paternal grandfather is a relation two degrees of consanguinity apart. Relatives in the third degree: great-grandparent, great-grandchild, aunt (who is a sister of parent), uncle (who is brother of parent), etc.

the *Troxel* case. In the *Troxel* case, the Supreme Court stated that parents have a right to decide with whom their child will have contact; in other words, it is up to the parents to decide when, where, and how the children will be allowed to spend time with a grandparent. In fact, the parents may decide whether the child sees the grandparent at all! A parent's decision to exclude the grandparent from a child's life is, by itself, unlikely to be reason enough for a court to find "significant impairment." Additionally, unique circumstances or serious signs of "unfit" parenting are usually necessary for a grandparent to win a possession and access case. Throughout my career I have represented both parents and grandparents on both sides of this issue. In some cases, I have had to appeal the erroneous rulings of trial judges to the Court of Appeals[23]. If you are a parent or grandparent and are facing a potential possession and access suit, you will need to hire an experienced, capable attorney who understands these unique requirements in the law and will fight for your rights.

---

[23] In re Sullender, 2012 Tex. App. LEXIS 5497; and In re Hogard, 2013 Tex. App. LEXIS 12631.

CHAPTER 10
WHAT AM I GOING TO DO ABOUT CHILD SUPPORT?

Under Texas law, both parents have a legal obligation to support their children until the child turns 18 or graduates from high school, whichever occurs last. There are other situations that may terminate the obligation to pay child support sooner, such as the death of a child, marriage of a child, etc. It is also important to understand that child support can continue for literally a lifetime if your child is "disabled," or if there is some special need for support to continue past age 18!

As stated earlier in Chapter 7 of this book, child support is unconnected to possession and access. And, as previously discussed in Chapter 7 of this book, even parents sharing 50/50 physical custody may be ordered to pay child support. However, a "non-parent" Conservator, such as a grandparent, can *never* be ordered to pay child support unless they adopt the child.

The Texas Legislature has mandated "legislative guidelines" in the Texas Family Code[24] which judges must follow when ordering the amount of child support a parent must pay. A judge cannot set child support at whatever amount they feel like just because they are a judge. If a judge departs from the legislative guidelines, then he or she must, if requested, explain their rationale in departing from the legislative guidelines. In my experience, most judges follow the legislative guidelines. Rarely is a parent benefitted by arguing for a higher payment of child support than normally assigned by the legislative guidelines. Likewise, it does not usually benefit the paying parent to argue that the child support should be lower than guideline amounts.

Child support payments are typically 20% of the net income of the individual ordered to pay child support for the first child and 5% for each additional child of the marriage or case. However, a parent already paying child support for children outside the current marriage, or court-ordered to support other children, may receive a credit based upon the number of other children the parent must support.

---

[24] These "legislative guidelines" can be found in the Texas Family Code at Texas Family Code, Section §153.251, and 154.121-22,154.125-26, 154.132-33, 156.402, and 154.406.

Multiple Family Adjusted Guidelines (% of Net Resources)								
	Number of children before the court							
		1	2	3	4	5	6	7
Number of other children the parent has a duty to support	0	20.00	25.00	30.00	35.00	40.00	40.00	40.00
	1	17.50	22.50	27.38	32.20	37.33	37.71	38.00
	2	16.00	20.63	25.20	30.33	35.43	36.00	36.44
	3	14.75	19.00	24.00	29.00	34.00	34.67	35.20
	4	13.60	18.33	23.14	28.00	32.89	33.60	34.18
	5	13.33	17.86	22.50	27.22	32.00	32.73	33.33
	6	13.14	17.50	22.00	26.60	31.27	32.00	32.62
	7	13.00	17.22	21.60	26.09	30.67	31.38	32.00

As of September 2018

Net income for purposes of calculating child support is not the same "net" printed on an obligor's[25] (parent ordered by a court to pay child support) pay stub. Rather, it is the net determined by the legislature, which is determined by a special calculation set by state law. The Texas Attorney General's office has an online child support calculator that you can use to calculate what your child support might be. The calculator may be found at: https://csapps.oag.texas.gov/monthly-child-support-calculator.

Each case is different and there are numerous rules and exceptions that apply, so you should not rely solely upon this calculator. With the assistance of your lawyer you can

[25] Obligor is defined as the parent ordered by a court to pay child support and/or medical support and reimbursement of medical, dental, and vision care expenses of a child.

successfully determine a more accurate calculation of what your child support should be.

It is important to remember that the non-custodial parent is also responsible for some expenses in addition to the required child support payments. These payments are typically ordered by a court as additional child support[26] that the non-custodial parent must provide. Typically, parents ordered to pay child support are also ordered to provide or reimburse the other parent, or the government, for providing major medical, dental, and vision insurance for the child. Sometimes a child receives government benefits that entitle the Texas Attorney General's office to seek reimbursement to the government from the non-custodial parent who is ordered to pay child support. The cost of insurance for the child (only for the *child* of the parties who are before the court) can then be deducted from the gross amount of the obligor's earnings *before* calculating the child support amount. This means that, potentially, an obligor not actually providing major medical, dental, and vision insurance for the child must send additional monies each month (in addition to the child support amount) to the custodial parent to "reimburse" the custodial parent for providing insurance that the non-custodial parent is obligated under the law to provide.

---

[26] See, Texas Family Code, Section §154.183- "Medical and Dental Support Additional Duty of Obligor". Vision expenses must also be paid as provided by subsection (c)(1).

In addition to the mandated insurance provision/reimbursement requirement, parents are also typically required to pay for all additional costs not covered by insurance, such as: co-pays, prescription drugs, or other "unreimbursed medical, dental, or vision care expenses,"[27] or procedures not covered by insurance. Although in most cases this splitting of expenses not covered by insurance is divided 50/50[28] between the parents, judges are authorized to order a different split or no split at all. It is possible for one parent or the other to be ordered to pay the entire amount of "non-deductible" expenses.

---

[27] "Deductible" as used in the insurance industry means: "The amount you pay for covered health care services before your insurance plan starts to pay. With a $2,000 deductible, for example, you pay the first $2,000 of covered services yourself. After you pay your deductible, you usually pay only a copayment or coinsurance for covered services." Source- www.healthcare.gov/glossary/deductible. "Unreimbursed expenses" is a term used in most divorce decrees, and SAPCR orders, to describe not only the deductible, but all amounts not actually paid for by insurance.

[28] See, Texas Family Code, Section 154.183., (c)

CHAPTER 11
WHAT AM I GOING TO DO ABOUT A MODIFICATION CASE?

Although the primary focus of this book is divorce and the questions you may have in contemplation of a divorce, you should be aware that once the Final Decree of Divorce is not necessarily the end of your case. Even after the final divorce papers are signed by a judge, both parents have the right to petition the court at a later time to "modify" the terms and conditions pertaining to child custody and child support. This request is called a Motion to Modify. You may petition to modify the order any time your circumstances change, even on a yearly basis, until your child reaches the age of 18. A child custody, visitation, or support modification may be ordered ***if***:

1) the circumstances of the child, or one or both parents, have materially and substantially changed, causing the current order to be unworkable or inappropriate;
2) and the requested modification would be "in the best interest of the child."

If a party wants to change custody of a child *within one year* of an order becoming final[29] Texas law requires that the party requesting the change sign an affidavit[30] stating facts and reasons why the change is necessary. The stated reasons for the change must prove that the current order is "seriously impairing the child's physical, emotional or psychological development,[31]" or must set forth that the child is above age 12 and will advise the court that they (the child) wishes to change custody. Another reason for changing custody in less than one year after the last order has been signed is that the parent in possession of the child has relinquished actual care, custody, and control of the child to

---

29 An order becomes "final" typically 30 days after the judge signs the order. During this 30-day period the order may be appealed. If no "Notice of Appeal or Motion for New Trial" is filed during this 30-day period, then the order becomes "final," and cannot be attacked.

30 An Affidavit is a legal document containing a statement by a person who declares under penalty of perjury what the witness has witnessed within their personal knowledge (seen and heard with their own eyes and ears).

31 See Texas Family Code, Section §156.102.(b)(1); See also, Sections: §102.004; §153.131; §153.432; and §156.006.

another person for more than six months. Texas case law[32] has established what *is* and *is not* considered a *serious impairment.*

If a person files a Motion to Modify within one year without attaching an affidavit[33] providing reasons for the requested change, the court is not permitted to take any kind of action regarding the requested modification. In the event a request is made for the court to change custody or change substantial rights and duties of a conservator at a Temporary Orders hearing, then the same affidavit is required. If the required affidavit is not filed, the judge is not supposed to schedule or conduct the Temporary Orders hearing. If your lawyer does not file the proper objection then even though the judge is not supposed to conduct the hearing, it may happen. Many lawyers do not know, remember, or understand this important detail, even though they are lawyers. Remember, what I said in Chapters 2 and 3, who you hire really does matter. I have, on several occasions, defeated a request to change custody or make major changes to rights and duties of a

---

[32] "Case law" is defined as: "the law as established by the outcome of former cases." Law in Texas is made by the three branches of government: legislative, executive, and judicial. The legislature (legislative branch) makes laws by introduction of legislative bills, debating those legislative bills, and voting to pass those legislative bills. After the governor signs the bill it becomes law. Law is also made by judges who "say what the law is" by rendering judgments or written legal "opinions" which contain the judge's Order/Opinion (judicial branch's) determination of what the legislature (legislative branch of government) intended or passed, and the governor (executive branch of government) signed into law.

[33] See footnote 27 and 28 in this chapter.

conservator because the lawyer representing my opponent did not know, or had forgotten this rule. You don't want to be in court (after having paid a lot of money to a lawyer) thinking you are going to win, only to get sent home quickly, with nothing, because you or your lawyer did not know about this rule and the other side did. Choose wisely who represents you.

A Texas child support order can be modified at any time after the prior order has become final, depending upon the circumstances. Circumstances which would constitute a modification include: a period of three years has elapsed since the original order was signed, the amount of child support has increased or decreased by 20%, or if the child support has increased or decreased by more than $100. Any parent, party, or the Texas Attorney General's office may petition the court to review the child support a parent has been ordered to pay. The Texas Attorney General is authorized to initiate a "review" of child support for either parent/conservator. Many fathers[34] do not realize they can seek help from the Office of the Texas Attorney General to initiate a review of a parent's child support

---

[34] Typically, it is the father who is the non-custodial parent and therefore the obligor ordered to pay child support. Under the U.S. and Texas constitution both sexes have an equal right to seek Conservatorship of their natural children upon separation. However, in my experience this typically means that the mother who usually has been the "primary caretaker" of the children is the parent most often awarded the status of Managing/Joint Managing Conservator, with the right to establish the domicile of the child(ren)=" custody. This trend is changing, slowly as more couples divide the child rearing duties.

order, whether the parent with custody of the child has requested a review or not. However, be careful to understand that the Office of the Texas Attorney General does not "represent you" even if they are initiating a review of your child support order at your request. They represent the State of Texas.

If you are a child support obligor and you lose your job, become disabled, or suffer some other interruption in your ability to earn your normal and customary income, you are entitled to seek a modification of your child support obligation. However, this decision should be weighed carefully with your own attorney, because there are both costs and benefits to seeking a reduction of child support because you can no longer afford to pay. Many persons ordered to pay child support simply stop paying child support when they lose their job or suffer some other interruption to their ability to earn a living. *Do not do this.* Failure to pay child support can subject you to fines, court costs, and jail, in addition to having to pay back what you owe, including interest! You may also have state issued licenses (law licenses, certified public accountant, etc.) suspended or revoked for failing to pay child support. You can even have your passport revoked. You have the right to ask for your child support be lowered if you cannot afford to pay what was previously ordered. In extreme circumstances, failure to pay child support may cause you to lose your parental rights.

CHAPTER 11

WHAT AM I GOING TO DO?
CPS IS AT MY DOOR

Because many divorces include children and child custody issues, I will discuss the role CPS may play in such a case. CPS investigations occur frequently in divorce and custody cases. Sometimes spouses or their extended family will file false reports of child abuse or neglect to gain an advantage in their divorce case. Often, the injuries commonly sustained by growing children, such as falling or scraping a knee, are blown out of proportion by a spouse or relative. Typically, these incidents are reported to CPS, in hopes of gaining an advantage in a custody battle or even custody itself.

Although it is illegal[35] to make a false report of child abuse or neglect to CPS, in my experience false reports are rarely prosecuted, and even more rarely punished. If you are being investigated by CPS, what should you do?

1. *Don't let CPS in the door—not even to look!*

If a CPS caseworker shows up at your door, ask specifically what they are there to investigate. Do not accept the answer of "abuse," "neglect," or any other generalized statement. CPS investigators are not police and therefore, *cannot* arrest you or take your child *without a warrant or court order*. Because CPS is not law enforcement, they do not have the right to enter your home without a warrant. The CPS caseworker wants to *get* information from you, not *give* information to you. *Do not let any CPS worker in your home for any reason.* There is no compromise on this. ***There are no exceptions.*** If you allow CPS into your home, *you have waived your constitutional rights* guaranteed to you under the United States Constitution[36]. If you

---

[35] Criminal law penalty-Texas Penal Code, Section §37.08 and Civil law penalty-Texas Family Code, Section §153.013.

[36] The 4th Amendment to the U.S. Constitution protects you from searches or seizures without a warrant. It reads, "The right of the people to be secure in their persons, houses, papers, and effects, against unreasonable searches and seizures, shall not be violated, and no Warrants shall issue, but upon probable cause, supported by Oath or affirmation, and particularly describing the place to be searched, and the persons or things to be seized." However, if you let CPS or Law Enforcement in voluntarily or upon their "request" then you have waived your constitutional rights. Law Enforcement and government agents like CPS are trained to "cozy" up to you and act

allow CPS to enter your home for any reason, *they will find something* in your home to justify a caseworker's biased, predetermined decision to remove your children from your home. The case worker may tell you "the Fourth Amendment doesn't apply to CPS," but that is a ***LIE!***[37] The caseworker may threaten to return with the police, and they might do just that, but it changes nothing. CPS and the police must, by law, have a warrant or a Court Order in order to legally enter your home. If law enforcement and/or CPS "force" their way into your home do not resort to violence! *Object to their entry* and use your smartphone to record the entire incident. Texas law allows you to record a conversation if you are a part of the conversation

---

friendly; or alternatively, intimidate you with threats; or even lie; in order to get you to let them in "voluntarily." There are little no ramifications for these lies or threats. Frazier v. Cupp, 394 U.S. 731 (1969), and it's prodigy of cases, hold that law enforcement may lie, and this does not invalidate a confession; "The fact that the police misrepresented the statements that Rawls had made is, while relevant, insufficient in our view to make this otherwise voluntary confession inadmissible. HN2 These cases must be decided by viewing the "totality of the circumstances," see, e. g., Clewis v. Texas, 386 U.S. 707, 708 (1967), and on the facts of this case we can find no error in the admission of petitioner's confession;" —Frazier, at 16.

[37] Child Protective Services Handbook, Tex. Dept. Family & Protective Services, **§2240 Interviewing, Examining, and Transporting a Child,** CPS August 2017, "The Fourth Amendment of the U.S. Constitution protects against unreasonable searches and seizures by the government. Caseworkers must comply with Fourth Amendment requirements when taking any of the following actions: • Entering a home. • Interviewing a child not in DFPS conservatorship. • Visually examining a child not in DFPS conservatorship. • Transporting a child not in DFPS conservatorship. Before taking any of these actions, a caseworker must have: • consent; • exigent circumstances; or • a court order."

being recorded[38]. You do not need to get anyone else's permission. You do not have to stop recording even if CPS or the police tell you to stop recording.

If the caseworker asks to come inside, politely decline. Hostility toward the investigator is considered evidence of guilt. You may be naturally angry about being accused of harming your child, but if you lose your temper or become hostile, it will be used against you as evidence of an "abusive personality." Even if the caseworker has a police officer with them, do not let them in your house. *Do not even talk to them!*[39] If a police officer is present, the police are most likely there for the protection of the CPS investigator. If they say they have a warrant, make them produce it and show it to you. If they refuse or say they do not have to show you the warrant, then advise them to get off your property. If CPS wants to talk to your children, you have the right to refuse. However, if CPS goes to the school or daycare

---

[38] Texas Penal Code, §16.02.(c) "It is an affirmative defense to prosecution under Subsection (b) that…(4) a person not acting under color of law intercepts a wire, oral, or electronic communication, if: (A) the person is a party to the communication;"

[39] See, "Don't Talk to The Police," https://www.youtube.com/watch?v=d-7o9xYp7eE". The information is also available in book format under the title, "You Have the Right To Remain Innocent," by James Duane, published by Little A, New York, 2016, Amazon Books. The book and video both include detailed real-life stories and reasons showing why you should not talk to the police or law enforcement without a lawyer.

and asks to speak to your child that is something they can do unless you are present at the school and direct school officials that you are opposed to CPS interviewing your child. CPS is not allowed to interview your child if you have advised them that you object to the interview and you are present with CPS when the objection is made.

2. *Take the charges made against you seriously.*

We have all seen news stories on television about the horrible abuse and neglect that some parents and adults inflict upon children. You must understand that it does not matter how ridiculous or unbelievable the story sounds to you. The caseworker is taking it seriously and so should you. Even though, under the law, you are innocent until proven guilty, this is *not* the practical reality. CPS case workers have admitted to presuming the people they investigate to be guilty unless there is evidence, they are innocent, or until the charges against the person are found to be false. You must understand that other parents have kept children in dog kennels or chained to beds, refused to feed and bathe their children, have beaten their children with baseball bats and water hoses, molested their children, and some have even sold their children for money to buy drugs[40]. You must

---

[40] Corpus Christi Mother Admits To Selling Her Children, Takes Plea Deal, Eleanor Dearman, Corpus Christi Caller Times, published 8:28 p.m. ET, April 5, 2019 | Updated 8:29 p.m. ET April 5, 2019, reprinted U.S. A. Today.

understand that when a CPS worker appears at your door, they do not know if you are like the people described above. Even if the caseworker says that they are not there to take your children, do not believe them! It is very possible that they intend to do exactly that, and you will be the last to find out.

3. *Record everything, but do it secretly.*

As I said earlier, it is not illegal in Texas to record a conversation, if you are a party to the conversation, even if CPS tells you that you are not allowed to record. But when you record, *do it secretly. Demand that all interviews between your child and CPS workers be recorded.* CPS is required by law to record "interrogations" (CPS calls them 'interviews') of children[41].

---

https://www.caller.com/story/news/crime/2019/04/05/corpus-christi-mother-admits-selling-her-children-takes-plea-deal/3376196002/

[41] Child Protective Services Handbook, Tex. Dept. Family & Protective Services, §2244.4 **Audio and Visual Documentation of a Child's Interview and Injuries to the Child,** CPS December 2017, "The caseworker must make an audio or video record of any interview with an alleged child victim or other child in the alleged victim's home in which the allegations are discussed, as appropriate for the child's age and development. The caseworker is not required to make an audio or video record if: • the child is unwilling to have the interview recorded; • the recording equipment unexpectedly malfunctions; or • the individual conducting the interview does not normally conduct interviews and does not have reasonable access to the necessary recording equipment.

The caseworker must attempt to take photographs of each child's appearance, injuries, lack of injury, and any other relevant evidence. If the parent is present, the caseworker must inform the parent of the intent to take photographs before photographing the child. The caseworker must not photograph the child if the child or parent objects.

The caseworker must never photograph a child's genitals except in the most limited circumstances. With a parent's consent, the caseworker may

Bring your own smartphone or other recording device just in case CPS "loses" theirs.

4. *Shut up and Listen!*

Don't talk to the police and don't talk to CPS. Keep quiet, even when you don't want to. It is absolutely essential that you do not answer *any* of CPS's questions until you have talked with your lawyer! You have a constitutional right to be represented by a lawyer of your own choosing. You have a right to your lawyer being present during any interview by CPS or the police. You may be tempted to defend yourself, but now is not the time. It is a natural feeling to think that if you are innocent you have nothing to hide. You may think, "I have done nothing wrong; what harm can come by talking to CPS"? (See, Page 109, footnote 27 in this book.) However, CPS caseworkers and police officers are not always reasonable. To them *the accusation is the evidence against you*. The case worker is there to find evidence to support what they already believe to be true: that you abused your child.

---

photograph a child's diaper area to document extreme diaper rash or injury in that area. Any examination or documentation relating to allegations of sexual abuse can only be done by a trained medical professional. Documentation If the caseworker is unable to make an audio or video record or take photographs, the caseworker must document the reason. Texas Family Code §§104.002; 261.302(e). The caseworker must use the recording software provided with her or his agency equipment. The recording must be uploaded into the agency's digital repository as soon as possible after completion. The most current upload procedures are located on the DFPS One Case: Functionality & Usage for CPS page. (accessible to DFPS employees only)."

You have a constitutional right to remain silent, *so use it*! If you give up the right to remain silent, then anything you say *will* be used against you. If you do not say anything to CPS, then you have taken away their greatest weapon: twisting your own words and then using them against you. If CPS asks to interview you or your child *refuse to do so.* Even if CPS has a warrant, that does not mean you have to speak to them or say a word about the accusations. Under both the U.S. and Texas Constitutions you are entitled to know the exact charges against you if you are accused of any crime. Your right to know the accusation against you also includes the specific details about what specific acts you supposedly performed which resulted in the injury or neglect of your child. "Abuse" and "neglect" are categories, not "details of acts." Insist on getting details!

You have the right to a lawyer of your own choosing, and you should exercise that right. A good lawyer will know what CPS legally can and cannot do. An experienced attorney will also know what kind of questions CPS can and cannot ask, and what evidence CPS can and cannot present in court. Find an attorney with experience *fighting* CPS. Many young and inexperienced lawyers begin their practice right out of law school by getting on the court appointed lawyer list. Although being on this list is not in and of itself a mark of a *bad lawyer*, many times these young lawyers do not have an established client base and depend upon appointments by the court to represent criminal defendants who cannot afford to hire a lawyer to acquire clients. I have seen these inexperienced lawyers get appointed by judges to represent parties in CPS cases. Often, when these inexperienced lawyers are assigned a CPS case, they lack the knowledge, experience, and courage to *fight* CPS. These court-appointed lawyers may have a lot of cases involving CPS, but because they depend upon the *system* to send them business. They do not fight for their clients, because they do not want to bite the hand that feeds them. I have seen these court appointed lawyers simply allow CPS plans, goals, and objectives, rather than challenging the allegations and digging up evidence to help you keep custody of your kids. You do not need someone advising you that is simply going to facilitate (help accomplish) what CPS wants to do to you and your children.

If the allegations involve physical abuse of your child, have your doctor give your child a thorough physical exam. Ask your doctor to then write a letter stating that no bruises, marks, or health concerns were found on your child that would create a suspicion of child abuse or neglect. Go to a doctor you trust. ***Never, never, never go to the doctor recommended by CPS!***[42]

---

[42]See, https://www.houstonchronicle.com/news/investigations/article/A-Devastating-Diagnosis-14419072.php;and https://www.houstonchronicle.com/news/houston-texas/houston/article/Doctors-accuse-moms-of-abusing-their-children-14492174.php; both of these stories detail recent circumstances in which "child

There have been many cases where doctors have been incorrect and, in some cases, have assumed there has been child abuse by a parent without following established medical diagnosis protocol and procedure. Some doctors have such a close working relationship with CPS that the doctors just assume that there has been child abuse, without medical proof, or in blatant disregard for other medical explanations of a symptom or injury.

Get your friends and family involved. Get the names, addresses, and phone numbers of friends and family who are willing to care for your children if CPS decides to remove them from you. CPS is required by law to place children who are removed with family or friends before considering foster care. If your children must spend time away from you, it is better that your children be around friends and family they have a relationship with and are comfortable with. There are many instances where children have been abused or even killed in foster care. Foster care is not a permanent solution.

Also, get your friends and family involved in your case by writing letters on your behalf stating what a good parent you are. CPS investigators are required to take such information into

---

abuse specialists" found "evidence of abuse." Both articles discuss how non-specialist pediatricians did not jump to conclusions because they were not *expecting* the parents to have abused the child and eventually ended up being integral in the restoration of the children to their families. Both cases talk about how the "specialists" often see abuse where there is none.

consideration, and it is much more difficult for them to illegally snatch your children without cause when they know that a crowd of interested citizens are watching.

Finally, *never, never, never admit to anything*, even if CPS has taken your children and promises to return them if you do admit guilt. If you admit guilt on any level, CPS will not return your children to you. If they were to return children to an individual who has admitted guilt, it would be a violation of their sworn duty. They are not above lying to you to prove that you are guilty of something, so do not trust what they say. They will not give you a break. They will use anything you say against you. Do not make it easy on them: keep your mouth shut. If you need to do any talking, let an experienced lawyer do the talking for you!

CHAPTER 13

What Am I Going to Do About Alimony?

The term "alimony" is often used interchangeably with the term "Spousal Maintenance," but the words are not synonymous, a fact which even some lawyers fail to understand or just do not know. In Texas, the term alimony has a different definition that spousal maintenance. *Spousal maintenance* is set by state statute, which regulates how much is paid, for a specific amount of time, up to a certain limit. Failure of a former spouse to pay spousal maintenance ordered by a Court to be paid can be punished by contempt of court. An agreement for periodic payments of spousal maintenance under Family Code Chapter 8, voluntarily entered into between the spouses and approved by the court, is also enforceable by contempt[43] against the person paying spousal maintenance. However, a court may *not* enforce by contempt a provision in an *agreed order* for maintenance that *exceeds* the amount of periodic support the court could have ordered, or that extends beyond the period of maintenance the court could have ordered under the law.[44]

Enforceability by contempt applies to enforcement of spousal maintenance and *not* to contractual alimony. Spousal Maintenance is money paid by one party to the other by virtue of a Judge's ruling. *Alimony* is money paid by agreement from one spouse to another and is enforceable as a contract; failure to pay *contractual alimony* is not enforceable by contempt because *contractual alimony* is considered a debt.

Post-divorce spousal maintenance is designed to be "remedial," meaning it is designed to "supplement" or "assist" a spouse after the divorce for a limited time. This spouse would be

---

[43] "Enforceable by contempt means that if a person is found to have disobeyed a court Order or Divorce Decree, certain provisions of Texas law allows the Judge to put the violator in jail and/or order the violator to pay a fine, as well as, pay the attorney's fees and costs of incurred by the person bringing the disobedience to the Judge's attention. Failure to pay a debt is not grounds for a Judge to sentence someone to jail or prison. However, certain financial obligations are not considered "debts" under the law. Therefore, in some situations such as failure to pay child support or failure to make certain payments under a divorce decree, a Judge may sentence someone who has violated the Order of the court to jail and/or order the person to pay a fine, court costs, and attorney's fees.

[44] See, Texas Family Code, Section § 8.059(a), (a-1).

disadvantaged by circumstances and otherwise unable to support themselves without some assistance from their spouse.

Just because a spouse qualifies to *seek* spousal maintenance does not mean they will automatically *receive* it. Unless a spouse seeking alimony does certain things and proves certain facts to the judge, they may not be awarded spousal maintenance. For instance, if while the divorce is pending the spouse seeking alimony fails (or refuses to really try) to get a job or to earn enough income for his or her basic needs, he or she may not qualify for spousal maintenance. Another instance in which a spouse would not receive spousal maintenance is if that spouse refuses to get a job or enroll in school that would ultimately result in the development of skills which would provide for his or her basic needs.

A judge may also consider several factors including the length of marriage, conduct during the marriage, and if any party or child of the marriage is disabled or in need of substantial personal supervision. Additional factors that influence a judge's decision to award spousal maintenance are the nature, amount, duration, and manner of the payments to be made to the requesting spouse. This includes an examination by the judge of each person's ability to provide for themselves, considering the spouses' financial resources on the date of divorce and the education and employment skill of the spouses. The judge will consider whether each spouse has sufficient education to earn themselves a decent living and if not, what amount of time will be necessary for the uneducated spouse to acquire sufficient education to get employment skills, or how much education or training is required to enable the spouse to earn a living. The judge also looks at the availability and feasibility (cost versus the benefit) of obtaining that education or training. The judge may also consider any property brought into the marriage by either spouse, the contribution of a spouse as a homemaker, marital misconduct (adultery, cruelty, etc.) by either spouse during the marriage, and any history or pattern of "family violence."

As stated earlier, the duration of the marriage is considered by the judge in deciding whether to order spousal maintenance. The judge also examines what effect paying spousal maintenance would have on the person ordered to pay, in view of all of the other things that person has to pay for, such as living expenses, child support payments and medical reimbursement. The judge can also consider things done by either spouse that resulted in excessive or abnormal expenditures, destruction, concealment, or fraudulent disposition of community property. Another factor for consideration is the contribution by one spouse to the education, training, or increased earning power of the other spouse.

Spousal maintenance begins typically upon the order of a court, which can occur at a Temporary Orders hearing or at a final hearing. Remember, Texas has no "legal separation." The closest thing Texas has which is comparable to "legal separation" in other states is "Temporary Orders." Therefore, if a spouse needs help in paying their living expenses, they can request "temporary spousal maintenance" be ordered by the Court, during the time the divorce is proceeding through the court system to a final hearing. However, such a spouse would have to demonstrate a need for it. It is important to understand that if the length of the marriage is too short to qualify for spousal maintenance it may still be possible for a spouse in need to obtain "*Temporary* Spousal Maintenance" during the period of time the divorce case is pending and being readied for final trial. However, there is a presumption in Texas that spousal maintenance should *not* be ordered. Unless the party seeking spousal maintenance presents evidence to the judge that rebuts the legal presumptions[45], discussed previously in this chapter, a request for spousal maintenance will not be granted.

Spousal maintenance is governed by Chapter 8 of the Texas Family Code and is set by law to be within certain ranges and amounts, depending on the length of time the parties have been married to one another, and the *gross* income the paying spouse receives. Notice that "spousal maintenance" is calculated on the "gross income[46]," which means income from any and all

---

[45] A fact, idea, or opinion assumed to be true under the law or legislatively enacted policy is called a presumption.

[46] See, Texas Family Code, Section §8.055.(a-1).

sources including wages, lottery winnings, illegal drug sales, and prostitution proceeds.

As stated in the last chapter, child support is calculated on the "net income" of the paying parent. However, spousal maintenance is calculated on the "gross income" amount. This means spousal maintenance is calculated on your income before taxes are taken out, and *before* "pre-tax" medical or retirement deductions are taken from your paycheck, spousal maintenance is calculated. If you are also paying child support, your spousal maintenance obligation will be calculated on the amount ***before*** your net income is used to calculate child support. Some people call this calculation difference an unjustified "double whammy." But justified or not, you must be aware of this significant difference. However, in no event will a spousal maintenance award by a Judge be over $5,000.00 per month[47]."

If you've been married at least 10 years but not more than 20 years, you can ask for spousal maintenance for a period of up to 5 years. If you've been married at least 20 years but not more than 30 years, you have the right to seek spousal maintenance for 7 years. If you've been married for 30 years or more, you are entitled to seek spousal maintenance for a period of 10 years. However, if

---

[47] Texas Family Code, Section §8.055(a).

the spouse seeking "spousal maintenance" is "disabled," the judge can order spousal maintenance for life[48]!

"Contractual alimony" is an agreement made between the spouses for the payment of alimony by one spouse to the other and there are no legal limits on the amount or the duration of such "contractual alimony." If you are representing yourself, be very careful if the subject of spousal support or alimony comes up. You may end up paying when you don't have to, more than you would have to, for a longer period, than you would have to. You may have heard the phrase, "You have to spend money to make money." Typically, board certified attorneys cost more than attorneys who are not board certified specialists. However, you should spend the extra money on a board-certified family lawyer, in order to keep (or get) as much of your money in a divorce as possible. This is especially true in cases where one spouse is seeking spousal maintenance.

[48] Texas Family Code, Section §8.054.(2).

CHAPTER 14

WHAT AM I GOING TO DO TO PROTECT MY ASSETS?

People contemplating divorce are also concerned about what will happen to their house, their business, their investments, and their retirement. Many times, people will attempt to move or sell assets, empty bank accounts, or use other means to prevent the other spouse from gaining access or control to valuable assets or accounts.

As I have discussed earlier and at length in chapters 5 and 6, most courts in Texas use what are called "Standing Restraining Orders" (SRO) in divorce cases. An SRO becomes effective as soon as the divorce is filed by the "petitioner." The spouse who did not file for divorce is the "respondent," and the SRO is filed against this person. These SRO prohibit moving or transferring assets, incurring new debts, and hiding or destroying property. They also regulate changing a child's residence or school, discussing the case with the child, and other conduct that should not be engaged in. It is not uncommon for people planning to leave their spouse to close bank accounts, move money to new "secret" accounts that the other spouse does not know about, check the children out of school and move to a new city or hide out from the other spouse, disconnect the utilities because they are in "their name", etc. Judges and lawyers call these type of actions "self-help" measures. It is this kind of unilateral action by one party against the other that courts try to discourage by issuing SRO's and TRO's.

Since standing restraining orders are effective as soon as the case is filed, people may inadvertently violate the order because they are unaware that the case has been filed. Once a person is aware that a divorce case has been filed along with a Standing Restraining Order, the SRO must be obeyed. Otherwise, a person violating the Is subjected to possible penalties of court, which could include jail time and a fine.

A Standing Restraining Order is effective once filed and a copy is provided to the non-filing spouse. Therefore, the sooner you file for divorce, the sooner you can obtain that protection. The date you file for divorce is significant because any changes made *before* filing are *not* in violation of the order, but changes made *after* the filing of the petition *are* a violation. The other party is automatically required to adhere to the terms of the SRO once they receiver formal notice of it, or they may be subject to fees or penalties as a result of a violation. In order to be held responsible for following a Standing Restraining Order, the court requires that notice of the SRO be "served" to the non-filing spouse. This notice can be delivered multiple ways, but the most common form of serving an SRO is to provide the recipient with a physical copy of the order. All "service" or official delivery of court documents must be done by law enforcement or licensed private process servers. A person contemplating divorce should consult with an attorney about how to protect their assets, in contemplation of divorce.

Although it is too late for anyone currently married, the best protection for from the ravages of divorce for one's assets and accounts is to create a "prenuptial agreement" *before* marriage. Generally, a prenuptial agreement can identify, segregate, and trace what is a person's "separate" property as contrasted with the parties "community property." In fact, prenuptial agreements can specify that the parties have agreed that there shall be *no* community property created during the marriage. However, after a pre-nuptial agreement is executed, its terms and conditions must actually be followed or the parties risk having "form over substance" and inadvertently "creating community property," which may destroy the entire reason for establishing the prenuptial agreement in the first place.

After the marriage has already begun, Texas also allows for the creation of "*post*-nuptial" agreements. A post nuptial agreement is an agreement made after marriage between spouses that allocate their property and how property acquired during the marriage will be characterized. However, these are not simply *pre*-nuptial agreements signed or executed after the parties are married. Some lawyers do not understand this difference, and the law has different legal requirements for *post*-nuptial agreements than for *pre*-nuptial agreements.[49]

Property owned by a person before marriage is that person's *separate property*. Property acquired by spouses during the marriage is presumed to be *community property* and must be divided upon divorce by the court. *Pre* and *Post* nuptial agreements can alter how this community property is titled, held, and ultimately divided in the event of divorce.

In Texas, the court is required to make a "fair and equitable" division of the marital assets. This is where suing for a divorce on a fault basis can make a difference If your spouse is found guilty of some fault, such as adultery, which results in the termination of your marriage, you may request the court for an unequal division of your marital assets. This means that, if your spouse is found to be at fault for the divorce, the court may divide your marital property *unequally*, so that instead of the customary 50/50 split, you may have a higher percentage of assets to which

[49] See, Robertson v. Robertson, 2017 Tex. App. LEXIS 11817, where a post nuptial agreement was held to be invalid because specific language required by statute was not included in the post-nuptial document.

you are entitled. The exact percentage of division is determined on a case-by-case basis. Some courts have divided marital estates unequally by rather large percentages, (80% to the non-offending spouse/20% to the offending spouse), and some courts have awarded even higher percentages!

Many different factors may affect the division of assets and debts in a divorce. "Fault" is the big difference maker in a divorce, especially when considering asset and debt distribution. Texas is a "community property" state, so any property that you own prior to marriage is your "separate property." In Texas, separate property is anything that you have received by gift, inheritance, or owned prior to the marriage. If you sign a prenuptial agreement, it is possible for parties to agree before marriage that they will never have community property and that what they purchase during the marriage will be one spouse's separate property or the other spouse's separate property. If you are contemplating a second marriage, I would strongly encourage you to consult a lawyer about the advisability of preparing a prenuptial agreement or doing some other form of asset protection.

Other factors that a court may consider in dividing the "community estate" are:

1. the disparity in earning capacity and business skills of the two parties of the marriage;
2. Age, physical conditions, and need for future support of the two parties to a marriage;

3. The relative financial conditions and obligations of each spouse;
4. The sizes of separate estates and any expected inheritance by a party; for instance, if you had a large separate estate, that may justify the unequal division of property in favor of your spouse.
5. Nature of the property awarded to a party of the marriage; a Court may consider the fact that one party to the marriage may be able to put a piece of property to use rather than sell it and divide the proceeds, since property sold at forced sale rarely brings its true value.
6. Wasting of Community Assets; a court may make an unequal award of marital property if one party to the marriage is guilty of "wasting" community property or assets. Recall the story I told you earlier about my client whose husband had been diverting ½ his monthly earnings into a secret bank account. According to the legal definition, that diversion of income would be considered wasting community property because the man deprived his wife of the use and enjoyment of his earnings which belong to the "community estate" within a lawful marriage.
7. Temporary alimony or support paid during the pendency of the divorce may also be considered by the court in making what otherwise would have been an equal division of the marital estate.

8. Gifts to spouse and children can also be considered by the court in making its division of the community estate. If community or separate property was gifted to a spouse or children during marriage, a court may consider these gifts in making its division of the remaining estate.
9. Tax consequences may also be considered by courts in making its division of the marital estate. The tax consequences stemming from a division of property as well as any unpaid tax liabilities incurred during the marriage are proper considerations to be made by a Court in making its "just and right" division of the marital estate.
10. Fraud committed by a spouse against the community estate can be considered by the Court in making an unequal division of the community estate. The theory behind this is to make the community estate whole by the unequal division.
11. Separate property used as a source of all community property can also be considered by a judge in making a "just and right division" of the community estate. If one party to the divorce used their own separate property as the source for a significant portion of the community estate, the court or judge may award a disproportionate property division in favor of the person who owns the separate property. You may inadvertently "co-mingle" separate estate property with community property. In the event of a divorce, you will be required to prove certain assets were owned by you before marriage, or that

certain expenditures were made from your separate estate accounts. If you are unable to unable to provide proof and documentation so that you can "trace" the flow of your money or assets, you may not receive a "just and right division" of what you brought into the marriage. It is *extremely* important to keep *separate property* separate and to keep accurate records of *what* you contribute to the marriage, *when* you contributed it, and the *circumstances* under which your contributions were made.

Typically, courts endeavor to do a 50/50 division. However, the facts of each case are different, and retirement benefits are, in large part, governed by federal law, which supersedes and prevents state court judges from making severe alterations. Under both federal and state law, there is a process for the court to divide retirement benefits. This process involves the submission of a signed order called a "qualified domestic relations order" (QRDO), which allows the division of federally controlled retirement funds in accordance with both state and federal law. The complexities that arise from division of marital property and the risks to your assets are just too great to not protect against having your property taken from you because you could not prove to the judge the contributions you made to purchase, maintain, or increase the property's value. To ensure that you keep what is lawfully yours, it is necessary to consult with an experienced, board-certified family law attorney.

Chapter 15

What Am I Going To Do Next?

In this book I have discussed divorce and the many decisions that lead to divorce and the many decisions associated with the process of getting a divorce. Divorce, like marriage, should not be entered into lightly. You should think long and hard before deciding what you will do and consider whether or not your circumstances will truly be improved by divorcing your spouse.

A study by the Institute for American Values, published in 2002, concluded that divorce or separation typically did not make adults happier than staying in an unhappy marriage. *The study concluded that "two out of three unhappily married adults who avoided divorce reported being happily married five years later*[50]." The study found that "unhappily married adults who divorced or separated were no happier, on average, than unhappily married adults who stayed married." The same study also found that "divorce did not reduce symptoms of depression for unhappily married adults, or raise their self-esteem, or increase their sense of mastery, on average, compared to unhappy spouses who stayed married." The study also found that "the vast majority of divorces (74%) happened to adults who had been happily married five years previously." The study found that "staying married did not typically trap unhappy spouses in violent relationships."

The Bible says in Proverbs 24:6, "for by wise guidance you can wage your war and in abundance of counselors there is victory." When I went through a divorce that I did not want, I took my father and one of my groomsmen from my wedding to interview lawyers. You need to surround yourself with people who love you and love you enough to tell you the truth even if it hurts or you do not want to hear it. Surround yourself with people who know you well, who you trust. Now, a word of caution: anyone can find a crowd to agree with them. People are, and public opinion is, fickle. So do not just listen to the largest group, the loudest voices, or the emotional pull—that is what a "mob" is.

---

[50] Does Divorce Make People Happy? Findings from a Study of Unhappy Marriages, Institute for American Values, ©2002, ISBN#1-931764-03-4.

You need to listen to people who know you like the back of their hand, people who are devoted to you and your success.

Most of all you need to get facts and sound legal advice. As I wrote about extensively in chapters 2 and 3, not just any lawyer, or the cheapest lawyer, will help you through the difficult process of divorce. Just because someone is licensed as a lawyer does not make them a good lawyer, and it definitely does not necessarily make them the right lawyer for you. You need to find a lawyer you can trust, a lawyer you can understand, and who treats you with respect and will listen to your concerns and desires. Finally, you need to find a lawyer with passion for your situation, your case, and your life. If you cannot understand what your lawyer is telling you, that is the first sign of trouble; find a different lawyer. How can you get help from a lawyer you do not understand…or who does not understand you?

After obtaining all the facts, and calculating the costs of divorce, both pro and con, discuss your options with your lawyer, and those around you that you trust. Be careful of who you talk to and what you say. You may unintentionally waive the confidentiality of your communications with your lawyer by telling other people what you and your lawyer have discussed. Make a principled decision based upon the facts, and the best advice and counsel. Life after divorce can be tough, and even with the best of lawyers and outcomes, you must tread carefully.

For those of you who read this book and believe in God and the teachings of the Holy Bible, know this: God loves all people, including you. God's word, written in the Bible, declares in III John 1:2 (ESV), "Beloved, I pray that all may go well with you and that you may be in good health, as it goes well with your soul." Whether or not a Christian should get a divorce is the subject for a different book but know that God will direct you if you call upon Him and obey Him. Jesus said, in Matthew 11:28-30 (ESV) "Come to me, all who labor and are heavy laden, and I will give you rest. Take my yoke upon you, and learn from me, for I am gentle and lowly in heart, and you will find rest for your souls. 30 For my yoke is easy, and my burden is light."

To qualify for God's help, you must believe that he is God, that he sent his son, Jesus into this world to die for your sins, trespasses, and wrongs, that Jesus rose from the dead, and ascended to heaven and is seated next to God the father interceding on those who believes behalf. In the Bible, the book of Romans 10:9-10 (ESV) states "because, if you confess with your mouth that Jesus is Lord and believe in your heart that God raised him from the dead, you will be saved. For with the heart one believes and is justified, and with the mouth one confesses and is saved." You must also follow the teachings of God found in the Bible, otherwise you cannot receive God's intervention into your life.

Jesus said, "If you love me, you will keep my commandments." John 14:15 (ESV). It is popular in our culture for people to demand the freedom to do what they want, and then at the same time claim the blessings, peace, and forgiveness that only comes when you actually do what God says. Often, I have found that the trouble in marriages can be attributed to one person, or sometimes both people, wanting what they want and being unwilling to yield to their spouse or, in some cases, even to God. This unwillingness to consider another point of view—the unwillingness to give up what one wants—is often the very core of the problem in a marriage, a business partnership, or any other joint endeavor. A healthy marriage is the result of work, effort, communication, and mutual sacrifice in pursuit of mutually valued goals and objectives. With a willingness to change, it is possible to learn new skills of communication and understanding, which combined with an unyielding allegiance to God, can save a marriage and make it successful. For couples who cannot or will not make this choice and change, divorce is available, along with all the potential issues discussed in this book which may follow the decision to proceed with divorce. Admittedly, divorce is a solution, but is it truly the best solution for you? God will direct you, if you read His word revealed in scripture. You do not have to travel this road of decision alone—and you shouldn't. Take the knowledge in this book, surround yourself with trusted advisors, and most importantly pray and ask God to answer your question, "What am I going to do?" This is what I did; when I went through a divorce I did not want (before I became a lawyer). God answered my prayers. God gave me this verse of scripture and I clung to it and it still brings me comfort today: ***"This poor man cried out, and the Lord heard him, And saved him out of all his troubles."***- Psalm 34:6 (NKJV).

Glossary of Terms

Acknowledgement of Paternity form: A form generated by the Texas Bureau of Vital Statistics where the father and mother of the child declare that they are the parents of a child. This form is typically used by parents who are unmarried to establish the fact that the man is in fact the actual father of the child.

Alimony: a husband's or wife's agreement in contract to provide for a spouse after separation or divorce. Alimony is distinguished from spousal maintenance in that alimony is an agreement between spouses as a matter of contract. Alimony is distinguished from "spousal support" in that "spousal support, either Temporary or Post-Divorce is an ORDER of the court that can be enforced by Contempt if it is not paid; Alimony cannot be enforced by contempt, except in certain circumstances.

Amicus Attorney: "Amicus attorney" means an attorney appointed by the court in a suit, other than a suit filed by a governmental entity, whose role is to provide legal services necessary to assist the court in protecting a child's best interests, while also representing to the court what the expressed desires of the child with respect to the litigation are, regardless of if the child's expressed wishes are in their best interest or not.

Attorney Ad Litem: attorney ad litem is "an attorney who provides legal services to a person, including a child, and who owes to the person the duties of undivided loyalty, confidentiality, and competent representation."

Case law: law established by judicial decision in prior cases.

Community debt: debt incurred by each of the spouses during the marriage.

Community property: property acquired by the spouses during the marriage, unless the property was by gift, bequest, or existed prior to the marriage.

Conservatorship: the status a natural parent or other person if so, ordered by a court, has in making decisions affecting their minor child.

Contempt: the offense of being disobedient to or disrespectful of a court of law. In Texas, generally, contempt of court carries penalties of jail and a monetary fine. In the case of civil contempt, it is possible for a person adjudged guilty of civil contempt of court to be jailed "until" they comply with the court's order that they have disobeyed.

Contractual alimony: alimony that a paying spouse agrees to pay to the former spouse, that is not necessarily Court ordered or is in variance from the statute or other limits on what a court is authorized under the law to order absent the agreement or contract.

Counterclaim: a cause of action brought by a defendant or other party, who has first been sued by the Plaintiff/Petitioner or some other party already a part of the litigation.

Custody Evaluator: a court-appointed mental health expert or an expert chosen by the parties, evaluates a family and makes a recommendation to the court for custody matters, usually including residential custody, visitation and a parenting plan.

Defendant: the name given to the person who is being sued by the person bringing the claim.

Deposition: The process of obtaining a person's sworn testimony outside of court, with no judge present. The deposition is recorded by an officer of the court, usually a "court reporter" and the recording is made by stenographic recording devise, which is then printed for use in a later trial or hearing. The deposition is used to establish a witness's testimony so that the witness cannot change their testimony at trial.

Discovery: the pre-trial process which requires parties to litigation to hand over information and evidence about a claim so all participants can know what they are facing at trial.

Estranged: a person who is no longer living with their spouse. no longer close or affectionate to someone; alienated.

Family Violence: (1) an act by a member of a family or household against another member of the family or household that is intended to result in physical harm, bodily injury, assault, or sexual assault or that is a threat that reasonably places the member in fear of imminent physical harm, bodily injury, assault, or sexual assault, but does not include defensive measures to protect oneself; (2) abuse, as that term is defined by law, by a member of a family or household toward a child of the family or household; or (3) dating violence, as that term is defined by law.

Final Decree of Divorce: court's formal order granting a termination of a marriage.

Fraud: There are different kinds of fraud, 1) Constructive; 2) Actual; 3) Statutory. If someone owes a fiduciary duty, they have a legal obligation to act in the best interest of another. When a constructive fraud claim is being alleged, the argument is that one spouse has a fiduciary duty to act in the best interest of the other spouse regarding the protection and management of the community estate, and that duty was breached by a spouse who misappropriated assets from the community estate. A constructive fraud claim can also be pursued under the theory of waste, where one spouse disburses community assets for noncommunity purposes without the other spouse's knowledge or consent. To prove actual fraud, a spouse must show the other spouse transferred community property for the primary purpose of depriving the claimant of the property with dishonesty or an intent to deceive which resulted in harm to the community estate. Statutory Fraud is fraud that is made illegal by a statute which usually prescribes certain penalties for the guilty party once a violation has been proven.

Hearsay: the report of another person's words by a witness, which is usually disallowed as evidence in a court of law.

Interrogatories: a list of questions one party sends to another as part of the discovery process. The recipient must answer the questions under oath. Because attorneys may help their clients answer interrogatories, interrogatory responses tend to be more finely crafted than answers to deposition questions.

Joint Managing Conservator: (JMC) is when the rights and duties of a parent are shared by both parties. However, exclusive right to make certain decisions (like where the child lives) may be awarded to one party. 1. JMC can be established either by an agreement from the parents or a court order.

Legislative guidelines: Guidelines for the calculation and payment of child support passed by the Texas Legislature into law. Judges are required to follow these guidelines in assessing the amount of child support for the number of children of the marriage as well as following the legislature's guidelines in other areas such as possession and access, called a Standard Possession Order.

Managing Conservator: The name given to describe a parent with rights and duties respecting their children. A managing conservator can be Joint or Sole. If Joint, both managing conservators can participate in making decisions regarding the child; if Sole then one parent or the other has the primary right to make the decisions regarding the child, exclusively.

Mediation: A process whereby parties to a lawsuit, with the assistance of a person trained in dispute resolution works with the parties to resolve their differences and achieve a settlement of their dispute or case.

Mediator: a person trained in dispute resolution procedures.

Motion to Modify: a motion filed with the court that seeks to change a previous court order or decree

Obligor: person who is court ordered to make payments of child support and/or spousal support.

Original Petition for Divorce: the initial petition that starts a divorce case.

Paternity suit: A suit filed to identify and legally declare a man to be the biological father of a child.

Petitioner: the person to begins a lawsuit in a family law matter. The term "plaintiff" is used in other civil cases to identify the person who brings suit.

Possessory Conservator: a person who has court ordered possession and/or access rights to a minor child. A possessory conservator can be a parent or non-parent. Typically, the "possessory conservator" is the parent or person who does not have day to day care custody and control of the child but has what most people call "visitation" rights to the child.

Post-Nuptial Agreement: an agreement made AFTER marriage by spouses that divides, conveys, or changes the characterization of that spouses' property.

Post-Divorce Maintenance: Court ordered payments to a former spouse for that former spouse's assistance in providing for that spouse's minimum reasonable needs after divorce. Post-Divorce Maintenance is limited in the amount of money and the length of time that a court may order the maintenance to be paid. Post-Divorce maintenance is often confused with "Alimony," which is not the same thing. Alimony is an agreement made between spouses for the payment of a specified amount of money for a specified period of time, by virtue of a written contract.

Pre-Nuptial Agreement: An agreement made between parties to an impending marriage, which sets forth the terms and conditions of how the parties will characterize their property, as well as other agreements affecting the marriage and in the event of dissolution, the terms and conditions affecting the division of property between the parties.

Qualified Domestic Relations Order: (QDRO) An order signed by the divorce court judge that provides for the division of retirement, pension, and other benefits pursuant to applicable federal law. This is a separate order from the divorce decree and should be pre-approved by the "plan administrator" before submission to the divorce court judge.

Request for Production of Documents: A document that commands a party or non-party to produce certain, documents, papers, and things. This is one of several different kinds of requests which opposing parties to litigation make upon each other to produce evidence relevant to the party's dispute or case.

Respondent: The person or entity sued. In non-family cases the term "Defendant" is used to describe the same person in other types of civil litigation.

Right to Determine the Domicile: The right under the Texas Family Code that is awarded to a parent or non-parent which enables that parent or non-parent to decide where the child subject of litigation to live. This right is the threshold right which gives a party "custody" of a child.

Rule 194 Requests for Disclosure: A discovery devise which requires the recipient to detail certain information about that party's legal theories, possible witnesses, experts, and other information they intend to use or which they contend relates to the law suit. Objections are ***not*** allowed to the Rule 194 Requests, which are a standard set of questions approved by the Texas Legislature to be reasonable and non-privileged information that all litigants are entitled.

Separate property: A spouse's separate property consists of:(1) the property owned or claimed by the spouse before marriage; (2) the property acquired by the spouse during marriage by gift, devise, or descent; and (3) the recovery for personal injuries sustained by the spouse during marriage, except any recovery for loss of earning capacity during marriage.

Significant impairment: What constitutes "significant impairment" of the child's physical health or emotional development is also not statutorily defined and must be decided on a case-by-case basis. Awarding sole custody to bipolar, violent father has been found to "significantly impair" child's physical health and emotional development. What is NOT significant impairment: evidence that child lacked sense of stability or family identity and had bonded with aunt.

Sole Managing Conservatorship: a parent or non-parent who has all the rights and duties of a parent set forth in the Texas Family Code, Section §153.132, to be exercised by that parent exclusively.

Spousal Maintenance: see, Post-Divorce Maintenance, this index.

Standard Possession Order: The minimum amount of possession that a parent or non-parent is entitled to receive for any child 3 years of age or older. Composed essentially of first, third, and fifth weekends of each month, a period of Thursday evening possession during the school term, and an extended portion of time in the summer, as well as, a portion of Holidays, and spring break. For parents who live more than 100 miles from the child a different standard possession schedule is available, if elected.

Standing: Standing, from the Latin phrase: locus standi, is the capacity of a person or entity to bring suit in court.

Standing Restraining Order: An order effective upon filing a lawsuit that prohibits the parties in a suit from doing certain acts, engaging in harmful conduct, destroying property, or refusing to do certain acts, that the court or local judges have decided by local court rule should be prohibited regardless of the facts of each individual case. A SRO, is like a Temporary Restraining Order, but different in that it applies to all cases whether or not it was requested by either party to a case, and is effective upon filing and service.

Statutory Rights: A right or series of rights that are conveyed by act of the legislature in law.

Suit for Grandparent's Access: Pursuant to Texas Family Code, Section §153.432., a grandparent may request Court ordered "access" or "possession" but not custody of their grandchild. However, one must essentially prove the natural parent of the child "unfit" in order to rebut the presumption in law that a Parent has the right to determine who has access and possession of their children, when, and at what frequency.

Suit to Affect the Parent Child Relationship: A suit filed, when parents are separated, that asks a court to make orders for the custody, control, possession and support of a child.

Temporary Order Hearing: A hearing held typically early in a case to decide issues needing immediate attention and service, on a temporary basis while the case is proceeding through the court system in preparation for a final hearing or trial. Temporary Orders can be heard on as little as 3 days' notice, and with leave of court, even sooner. Temporary Orders once made last until modified by the court, final hearing or trial; which can be for years.

Temporary Restraining Orders: A temporary restraining order, commonly known as a "TRO" is used in civil law cases, which includes family law, to place injunctions without a full hearing on one or both parties, for a period of 14 days, during which time a hearing is held to determine if the injunctions (restrictions) should continue. These injunctions prohibit specific actions that could endanger or prove damaging to the property in a divorce or the children of a divorce. After a hearing is held where both sides can present their reasons for and against the TRO continuing, a court can dissolve the TRO or convert the TRO into a Temporary Injunction, which although it has a different name is essentially the same thing, just not limited to a 14-day period like a TRO.

Third degree of consanguinity: Two people are related to each other by consanguinity if one is a descendant of the other or if they share a common ancestor. An adopted child is considered to be a child of the adoptive parent for this purpose. Example: Person A is related by the third degree of consanguinity to person B if person B is person A's uncle (brother of person A's father) because they share a common ancestor. However, person A is not related by consanguinity to person C if person C is the uncle's spouse, because person A and person C share no common ancestor.

Waiver of citation: Waiver of Citation waives your right to be formally served with the divorce or lawsuit papers. A waiver of citation typically does not waive any other rights, however, in some circumstances and depending upon how the waiver is drafted, you can give up other rights you would normally have if you had chosen to be served and appeared in court for hearings. Filing a waiver can be like giving your spouse a blank check, allowing them to go into court and get what they want, how they want it, when they want it, with no further notice to you.

Wasting: "Waste" occurs when a spouse spends money or uses property for an improper purpose during a marriage. A spouse in a marriage can allege "waste" if assets, or money, were spent on things which did not "benefit" the community estate of the marriage. For instance: spending money on a girlfriend, a secret gambling habit or illegal drugs. Unfortunately, not all losses by a spouse are regarded as waste. Spending too much money on legitimate activities (such as shopping, hunting, or golf) will not be considered “waste” by a court even though you may consider such over-spending to be wasteful.

INDEX

O

P

R

S

T

NOTES

Made in the USA
Las Vegas, NV
03 November 2026

57425294R00095